D1063200

Train
River
Poetry

anthology

THANK YOU

We would like to extend a special thank you to our incredible Supporting Members who make our publications possible. With their support we have been able to build incredible contemporary anthologies.

SUPPORTING MEMBERS

Eileen Wiscombe
Annie Percik
Jenni Jolly
Lana Hechtman Ayers
Lauren Michelle
Stephanie Robertson
Sian Maciejowski
William Falo
Marcia Knight-Latter
Karl Kadie
Elizabeth
KC
Jessica
Anonymous

Barbara Soehner
Tanja Krstulovic
Jessica Bullard
Amelia Robyn
James Goggin
thewhite.m05
Joan Gerstein
CEC Haydon
Sam Piscitelli
Leon Gregori
Dakota Avellino
Marie Claire
TazThePoet

We look forward to continuing to grow and publish more poets and authors. Thank you for joining us on this journey.

fall 2020

Patch
the medøchï

In anger I was told,
"You reap what you sow."
Yet it is I, who rests here in peace.

I had to breathe life into that
corpse, and quilt together a broken soul.
Piece
by
piece.

@themedochi

Grandmas Words
Joanne F. Blake

Didn't understand why she kept
the bible in her hands
Didn't understand why she said
never trust the man
Didn't understand why she stayed
on bended knee
Didn't understand why she
prayed for me
Grandma spoke words
my ears didn't hear
Tried to prepare me
for when the end was near
Now that I think, I should have
left the cookies and the candy
and picked up the words, that
Grandma tried to hand me

@joannethepoetess

i want what i need, i need what i want.
Jaden Ogwayo

i want to stop enduring this same pain day in, day out. i want to let others know that i inherit the screams of my murdered brothers and sisters without being called 'pressed'. i want to see change and not just a repost of another video of another black teenager getting shot. i want to wear my skin tone with pride but i fear a uniformed officer will see my complexion as permission to kill. i want to exist without being mistaken for indigenous and contributing to the fact that aboriginal children make up half of imprisoned youth. i want to drive without being pulled over and forgetting to film the seconds before i suffer an act of violence. i want to see tweets of donation and petition links so we can fund protestors' bails. i want my time line to stop being a cemetery for the fallen names uncovered by the media. i want to protest. i want to scream. i want to scream until my vocal chords give out because the victims of this shit can't. i want to riot. i want to steal. i want to loot. i want to advocate for those whose breaths were stolen by coward cops. i want to see change. i want uniforms to stop camouflaging killers from the justice system. i want to protest. i want to cry of rage, not from tear gas. i want the tears in 'tear gas' to be tears cried for george floyd. for breonna taylor. for elijah mcclain. for the other victims of this shit whose stories weren't viral enough to be memorialised as a hashtag or captured on tape. i want to anticipate the end of police brutality, not wonder when I'm next. i want black lives to start mattering, and blue lives to stop murdering.

@jadenwrites

His Name is George Floyd
runawaywriters

Black bodies don't hang
from oak trees anymore
they lie flat against
hard concrete floors -
on public streets
completely unarmed
under the weight
of an officer's knee

@runawaywriters

No Love
Joanne F. Blake

What gives you the right
to turn off another's light
No love, no life
no chance to breathe
Only tears from a family
left to grieve
I just wanna breathe

@joannethepoetess

this country will breathe again
with new hands to protect it
Kara Murphy

empathy will heal
the nation that's been
suffocating underneath the
hands of the egocentric
and heartless.

@poet.inthemaking

Little Black Crow
Kimberly Boateng

"My little black crow dear why are you crying"
Well my nest got destroyed and my children are dying
They washed out our tree
And cut down my park
Dear dove I am here, this is why I am crying

"My little black crow, so your children are dying
So you sit here with me doing nothing but crying
Well I'll share you some knowledge you little black crow
Here are some things a black crow ought to know"

Knowledge you say
Said the little black crow
Please help, I beg, I'd like what you know.

"Well my dearest black crow
What you ought to know
Is the little blue birdy is down by the trough
The neighbors are there
And they're taking good care
They are very busy helping I'll have you know"

Helping who? Squealed the little black crow
I am the one who needs help what don't they know
Little blue birdy is safe and sound
While my dearest little children become one with the ground
Please my dove this is not only a show
Us crows need help said the little black crow

"How rude of you, you incessant crow
I told you everything you ought to know
Little blue birdy is important too
You mustn't think you're all that because you're just not blue
Now keep quiet you little black crow
We're busy doing things that a crow mustn't know."

With that, the doves shooed away this sad little crow
To seek some help it continued to go
Flying low
With nowhere to go
Still crying
And its children still dying
The little black crow

@k.agyeii

i thought you're here to protect us?
Colleen Tubungan

hiding behind a see through responsibility,
teared up gas leak from the roof of humanity.
we can't allow to breathe in your toxic norm routines -
call it martial law, nodding of heads and kissing shoes of
the fiend.
but you see, we're not foolish enough to stick in oppressed
fear
so you call us a riot and you call for more back up badges.
you resolve peace with nothing but bullets.

@lostandstars

To Every Brown Girl and Boy
Meresa Harley

From a young age
We learn about race
What we can do
What we can't
We learn our "place"
We come in all different shades
We stand out
When we speak up
We get shut down
We struggle,
We are calloused,
They are privileged.

Despite the cards we've been dealt,

We aren't a statistic
We aren't a headline
We aren't a minority

And the birth of your existence
Was not the death of your opportunity.

@melanatedmagic.poetry

The Ghetto
Yasmine Ahmed

My home has split personalities.
In the winter it is quiet.
Not much moves other than the dead trees that sway with
the wild breeze,
And the squirrels that run around searching for something
that they and I both know they will never find.
Not much occurs, and everyone stays hidden in their
homes.
I guess it's because black people don't do well in the cold.
But in the summer, it comes alive.
It is loud, extravagant, and warm.
Everyone takes all the energy that they compiled from the
past months of solitude,
And unleashes it onto our streets all at once,
In the form of parties, games, and the smoking of blunts.
The kids would roam the streets,
Condensed into packs of kinky hair and dark skin,
Playing games, racing bikes, and ringing doorbells only to
run away.
They plan their future away from our mirage of a home,
Surrounding colorful playgrounds with harsh gravel
perfect for scraping knees.
My home is welcoming to all, with the exception of the
men in uniform.
It can be heard far and wide with its cultured music and
gunshots.
The shots did not intrigue me as much as they did the
other kids.
They seemed to be drawn to them, like moths to prisons.
The transformation was one that I expected.
It is the same transformation that happens to most that
stay here.
It starts off with the small things,
The missing bike stolen by one of the bad boys.
But those bikes then turned into cars,
And those summers of us playing manhunt as kids,
Transformed into their own personal game of manhunt

with the men in uniform.
They seem to have forgotten about our plans to escape the moment they lit their first joint.
My home never ceases to amaze me with its minimal twice annual gathering of these uniformed men.
Searching for stolen cars, drugs,
Or investigating a murder.
How our lives have changed,
From winter to summer,
We look different,
We feel different.
From kids to criminals,
We experience the loss of innocence, lives, and hope,
All within our neighborhood,
Or simply, within our hood.
It's crazy to think about how we can strike fear into the hearts of others simply by saying our street name,
And how our address to a man in uniform is an automatic reason to be suspicious of us.
To them, it is a ghetto,
Incomplete within itself.
Filled with violence, crime, and those who will amount to nothing,
Those who are you and me.
But to us, it is our home,
Where we grow and experience.
But most of all,
It is the place that we try to escape,
For a better future,
Because there is no future here for us.

@_yxsmine_a

I Pledge Allegiance
Khari Rice

Here is a letter to your flag
land of the free, home of the brave
body shackled to the pavement just to watch that banner
wave
I pledge allegiance to my grave,
set out just for me
Born with a target on my back
but that's your claim of liberty,
your praises of equality
But how can you expect them
to embrace a land whose foundation was
built on the backs of my ancestors
& still aint meant for me?
still aint meant to be
free
I mean

I pledge allegiance to my black,
for which I choose to save
But your white privilege,
blue uniform and blood red stain's engraved
into the concrete for which I lay
One nation under God
I've never hated a set of colors as much as I do these
givin' you permission to cuff me up & beat me to my knees

I pledge allegiance to my body,
the way we chant that "black don't crack"
& yet you shatter my melanin all over these streets
just like broken glass
I was a mirror
who reflected the past
of whom had hoped for a better tomorrow
But instead, my mother is forced to memorize my eulogy,
pen a will I didn't create,
forget ever seeing me walk down the aisle on my wedding
day

9

You pledge allegiance to the stars you branded into my
skin
with 13 stripes around my neck that seem to have no end

I pledge allegiance to my life,
one taken by that gun,
to fight for your liberty and justice...
Congratulations,
you've won.

@brownsugasoul

the medøchï

They used to tell me I wasn't black,
because they couldn't call me a hoodlum.

They used to tell me I wasn't black,
to mold the way I'd act.

They used to tell me I wasn't black,
until they saw how a stranger cop would react.

They used to tell me I wasn't black,
until they want a nigga to have their back.

They used to tell me I wasn't black,
when those I.Q. tests said they never reached where I was
at.

Now they ask how is it to be black,
so here's my answer.

Lies about your existence is just a little white fact.

@themedochi

before the winter comes again
Ava Silverman

March was for the panic,
April for relief,
May for revolution,
June a promise that we'll keep.
July will be rejoicing,
not a party, but a start.

//

August will be goodbyes,
to ring in new beginnings in
September
where we'll treasure the days
before wintry weather
once again cascades
into our valley of hope.

@make_the _flowers_grow

20/20 Vision
Joanne F. Blake

I thought the blood saved our lives
and meant that we were free
Today we're living in a world
that's afraid of unity
Color is now an issue
people fighting over tissue
I can't believe in 20/20
this is the vision
that we see through

@joannethepoetess

why am i an immigrant?
Shanai Tanwar

why am i an immigrant
and you an expat

there is a word of difference
between you and i
and that is enough
to cover the distance
between here and home

a home where
my father had two degrees
and this foreign land where
he is paid in
half promises and little regard
because his accent doesn't
warrant higher

@inkbyshanai

the colour of language
Tanya Sharma

immigrant child
whose love language
for so long
has been the
translation
of white words
into mother tongues
for those who
gave you
this life

you are the product
of your
incredible ability
to harness
all the colours
presented to you
in a way that
has allowed you
to thrive.

@powertovoices

The Caffeine Falls
Caleb Knight

I cascade down
the Caffeine Falls,
and by noon I'm lying
face down at
the bottom of
a lake.

My legs are crammed
beneath a desk
barraged by sticky notes,
like I'm working on
the battle map
of the Capitalist Agenda.

I want freedom!
To soar outside
relieved of all my duties;
to live again
the outstretched days
of Childhood's Eternity.

Who made me sit here?
Who told me my value's
the money that I make,
the tasks that I complete
within the Nine to Five
of every day?

Nobody knows I'm
poeticizing
the hours of my lunch break.
I can't exist solely
inside words writ on a page,
but this Vast Expanse
allows me my escape.

@summerofcaleb

that one friday night
René Camus

we laid on a crack-filled
suburb sidewalk
away from the blaring horns
and heavy sighs of rush-hour
trafficked highways—
too beaten to get up
from the haze of a good time.

I don't remember why we
were drinking in the first place.
was it to forget?
to celebrate?
or did we just drink
to make things happen
because nothing was?

all I remember
was passing a Friday night
just lying on our backs,
sucking on booze, and counting
the bulletholes in the sky—
mindless of what people think.

in a city where lost souls
pretend to be found,

that evening was as good
as it could gets.

@renecamuspoetry

Wild Ivy
Shristi Das

Wild ivy bloomed in my heart, re-attracting those swallows
to my chest,
They nestled in the warmest corners, of this desolate home,
sucking nectar out of the pain, I hid away long ago,
doing what they do best,
Flapping their majestic azure wings vehemently,
they summon tornadoes,
picking up,
gathering,
taking away,
every bit of malice and cruel intentions I had ever
harbored,
I close my eyes and count to five,
1
  2
    3
      4
        5
Bearing fruits poisonous to my body, yet essential to them,
made me feel so alive,
In fact,
Acting as a stand in for mother nature,
They let me feel a sense of divinity,
I never felt before,
Leaving my soul behind, unscathed,
the love within me lingered on,
Waiting to germinate,
Like a powerful, dormant spore

@peachteamusings

A poem after I declared
myself a Nautical Renegade

Benidamika Jones Latam

I have always been afraid of the sea,
that is why I eat a handful of salt before going to sleep.
I wash my hair with brine for a weak smell of the beach,
I practice carving crystals out of white rocks -
the only mental image left of you reduced to a coral.

September 9th, the day the waves came to pick you up,
I think it swallowed my heart along with your goodbye -
clung to the two syllables like anchors on a shallow shore,
its feet resisting the slippery sand
turning the deep blue a murky grey.

If you throw a lovesick heart into the ocean
it will bleed till the second coming, and the second coming
came
because of it, the seas have changed colors and god wants
to undo it
but there are no time machines in heaven.

Right before the second coming;
the fishes, plankton, and two million undiscovered species
hated me
for one second. They hated me for birthing Armageddon
when I lost you
they didn't know me, but if they did
they would understand why I spent hours deep diving my
worst fear
in hopes of finding you, I rocked the boat back and forth
till my arms grew heavy without the weight of you.
Your absence is a tremendous loss
and it would've pulled the sky under the sea if He wasn't up
there.

I spent months at sea waiting.
Waiting for -
glassy eyes, a mirror, a window, anything transparent -

anything for a hint of you.
I waited.

The spells of sea salt made me brain-sick,
I waited for my body to morph into a fish
I yelled, "there's nothing romantic
about mermaids and lost souls, sinking souls,
drowning lungs and fallen angels."

I declared myself a nautical renegade and waited
for my set of gills but they never arrived,
the delivery boy called and said, "the sea is not a valid
address."
I spat on the liquid ground and screamed, "WHY
HAVE YOU NEVER BEEN KIND TO ME?!"

The sea has never held me in her arms, even when I asked
her to
but she took you in, like a stray
chained you around her neck with a seaweed locket
and a pearl in your mouth,
she made it soft
when your head hit the seabed.
She let you sleep.

Months after she took you, I stopped going to the beach
I'm jealous.
The seashores sing lullabies for you.

@chasxng.auroras

Sunset Palette
Sophie Cook

at the banana tree
I inspect each bruise
on the bright yellow palette
I feel a subtle jealousy
the bruises, they make them more ripe
just before they rot away
banana peel cannot be sewn back on
once we remove each strip, one by one
when you undressed me
you couldn't keep it all to yourself
if I ever managed to take it all back
you'd see each bruise
almost covered
my bright yellow colour muddy brown
am I ripe enough?
or are you done with me now?
discarded, at the bottom of the banana tree
your carelessness looks for another to eat
see, I can't even sit at a banana tree
without feeling like you peeled
each part of me away
bruised, but once perfect I sit
facing what you have done
unable to cover what you did
at the banana tree, in the sun
s.c

@writingsophie

19

Braiding her hair~ Sunday afternoon
JYOTSNA MOYEE DAS

hair is a cliché
yesterday's stick to it
stories are jumbled
rolled behind ears
brushed by fingers
the glitter patches on nails
snuggles and seeps into skin

often try to rinse and
give the present a new definition
braiding hair does not help
charms and jingles
sorrow and malice
sway like tides
enchanted whispers chasing my ears
eventually bringing tears.

@jyotsna.moyee

wonderful
Teodor Nihtianov

the wine is good tonight
and the city fumes are floating
through the window
we don't have a record player
so we hum, like little earthquakes

the sorry souls outside would be jealous
if they could peek through our windows
but they keep walking, thumping the cement
and we keep singing
secret songs, familiar melodies

@twistedprusti

Ordinary days of an extraordinary love

Simon E. Northcott

Unkempt hair
And no make up.
I love your lazy
Days of unmade bed,
Junk food and piles
Of dishes in the sink.

When you dance and all
The steps are wrong, the
Window open and you say
Stop. I call you Baby
And you laugh and laugh
And laugh and my heart
Is ready to explode
With love.

simone.northcott

Helena Kobayashi-Wood

Her mother disliked the mess of a child
So much that the girl had to eat ice cream in the bath
Followed round with baby wipes
Until she begun to police her own sticky palms

She stopped colouring
Too scared she'd ruin the pictures
Washed her hands so often while painting
That she ran out of time to form a complete picture
Ran out of time to just be a child

No matter the amount of soap or wipes
She was always just a little too sticky
Her hair out of place
Her voice too loud
Her shoes too scuffed

She did her best to please
But somehow her best was
Never
Quite
Enough
Until she realised that the only person
She needed to be enough for
Was herself

@the.light.of.living

Love & Life

James Goggin

One day I'll be 100
And I'll have read all the books,
And bedded countless beautiful people,
And I'll be celebrated for having written
Something good that managed
To make a little noise.

I'll be the spiritual twin of Ram Dass
With a clear Buddha mind and a pure
Christ heart. I'll be a philosopher king
Walking across fire and breathing in
The mountains, and the stars, and the death,
And the like. I'll be the greatest version
Of myself I could ever hope to be.

One day I'll be 100
And drinking with a fellow centenarian
That I've known since birth
And they'll say "Jim
You haven't changed at all."

We'll both laugh and my ego
Will fall apart like a glacier in July.
What a fabulous journey
I am on.

@barfly_poetry

23

5 AM
Berly Rivera

enveloped in white cotton sheets,
i close my eyes and tune into the sounds of early morning

the chirpy chatter of the morning birds,
eventually, it subsides and i figure their conversation is
over

the soft tick-tock of the gray alarm clock,
it rests on the sill of my open window

the whispered whoosh of artificial air,
escapes a vent that's just a tad out of my reach,

a gentle inhale and exhale of breath,
eventually, i am lulled back to sleep

@wordsbyberly

CEREZAS
Michelle Gerrard

He tasted tart and sweet
Summers first cherries laced on his lips
Crimson kisses traced down my neck
As I looked up at the egg yolk moon that shimmered on the
water below.

Dust became sapphires with every touch.
You
Were an alchemist of feeling.
The way you enticed my senses to awaken
Electric pulses of life cascading like dancing lights on a
still sea

I always thought I would rise into another
Who embodied the flow of water
Sea salt traces on bare skin
The memory of the way he would bend around every curve.

And yet here I am with your immovable earth.
Roots that bury into stone
Eyes as steady as a rising sun
Bright and fervent with an enduring serenity.

I always thought I wanted pomegranate kisses
Hidden passion intertwined with agony.
When under the secret of that moon , I secretly craved
cherries,
Warm from the glistening sun
A sweetness that lingered.

@michelle.nicole.gerrard

It is a statement shovel
Sara Farooqi

The shovel has been in the garden for a few weeks now

It says
Look at this tree where I rest my head
Its flowers blooming in the oblivious spring sun
And three bird feeders sway with the pulse of the wind
Whose endless seeds have welcomed regular guests
The same robins, blackbirds, sparrows
Even squirrels all feed in unconventional alliance
There is less around me
But I see more, so much more
I can just watch the birds
I'm fine, believe me

And look here, to my left
The rustic vegetable patch that I have built
With wood scraps and soil from the garden
Everything that I needed was already here
And do you see?
The chives, onions, carrots, already stretching to the sky
And soon, soon
I can eat the fresh vegetables I have grown
I can be self-sufficient
See, if anything happened, I wouldn't starve

Honest, I don't need much more
From the world beyond this garden
I am okay
    I am okay

@s.n.farooqi

May
jess denman

sometimes we talk
of nothing
and sip lemonade
under a new moon
as night would fall

May brought longer days
with you

@j.maye_

beliefs
Kim Backalenick Escobar

not everything at the dollar store costs
a dollar/so i don't know what to believe
any more/i was raised by an atheist and
an agnostic/and i have followed in their
footsteps/so i'm a definite maybe when it
comes to faith/i have faith tomorrow will
come/there will be flowers/someone will
cry/laugh/die/i believe there have been
wars/bloodshed/over religion/and borders/
and useless ideas/babies will be born/and
some will find smiles/i believe if you
hold a buttercup/under your chin/and it
looks yellow/that you like butter/knocking
on wood is important/and finding a four
leaf clover is almost impossible/so it
must mean something/

@edgeofpoetry

Anxiety Study
Melissa Felson

like memorizing the remains of you through a
closing door

like pitted stone fruit,
all split open and dripping mess

like slow bloom of stress pimples along my jaw

like when did I become -
glass figurine
hummingbird hands
misfit heartbeat
and fists on ribs

like all-caps FRAGILE in red box-letters

like every time my dad left he had to say goodbye,
so I'd remember
the last words
he'd said to me

like the time he didn't, on purpose
to help me break the habit

@intotheminefields

Autumn leaves
Vibhor Kathuria

The first thought, in a refreshing morning
Autumn leaves are crawling by wind
It's been ages, not literally but it seems
like that, as time is stuck in random pages
of 1Q84, never ending
but still progressing
Bringing out a refreshing
morning, once again, and everyday.
Birds didn't chirp today, it's lost
Like the shine of the sun,
the voice, now don't ring the eardrums
or are the ears shut down?
because not listening makes forgetting easy.
Forgetting the whoosh, and the tick tock
Still lies the mystery,
What was the first thought?

@the_elegantscribe_

THE HARE MOON
Charlotte of Shalott

nothing but blackness remains.
the shadow of her promising light
that had us infused for a glorious
split second
where we were found and cradled and things returned
to their right places —
it was but a flicker of hope
a glimpse of power
a weak-willed indulgence
in incandescent decadence.

she has left. like so much leaves and betrays and forgets.

nothing but blackness remains.
this most capricious mother
has forsaken these would-be children of hers
this love of change is questionable
(enviable)
I had stabbed her gently in the face and she bled
no more than drops
of her light into our pretty shells, handpicked,
guilt-ridden, dignified
still my arm reaches upward
still my elbows twist hideously from the strain
of my leaden will
still skin stretches tightly over my wrist
sinews straight like strings on a violin
waiting to be plucked
waiting for a bow to bring them back
to life in a vibrato shudder

nothing but blackness remains.
remains. the comfort of the word nestles neatly into my
secret
sentimentality,
my clandestine melancholy,
its intrusion sensed by a nagging voice from the pit

of my stomach, hoarse with the sleep
of centuries
it rises in me like rage and gall and compunction
taunting me with the possibility
of futile unknowns and lofty spheres, an even greater
perhaps than this
i watch the train
of her incantatory utterings,
the same simple phrase repeated, waxing,
waning, and waxing again
and close my nystagmic eyes
against the force of it,
suppress it, allowing no distractions
from the structured devotion.

but the knowing remains.

i shall whisper it into the woods now
to be rid of it,
bury it in the blackness
of this night sky womb.

it remains to be seen
what she shall birth from it

@charlotteofshalott

The speech Nixon would have given if Apollo 11 had failed on July 19, 1969

Camden Michael Jones

These brave men,
Dick Nixon would have transmitted
across the nation
on July 20, 1969
if the moon lander
had failed to liftoff from the dust
    will be mourned
    and their sacrifice remembered
but of Neil and Edwin
the people would have
traced them in the night sky
as constellations of flesh.

    In their exploration
    of that veil,
the words would have trickled
into the lander cabin
stranded on the surface
    these men paved a tomorrow
    for others
and waited for the electric click
to signal the end of transmission.
The blood in those lonely bodies
might course in earnest
as though in defiance
of impending starvation
or asphyxiation,
as though a beating heart
could stave off vacuum
and the cold slipping silently
into their limbs.

    For us who look up at the moon
    in nights to come
and feel the weight of above,
we will know

there is a corner
of someplace else
that shall forever be mankind
    let us commend their souls
   to the deepest of the deep
    and bid them farewell
    on their next journey.

@camden.m.jones

the medøchï

They prayed for rain
to wish their sins away,
but a sun shower occurred.

So to cleanse, their dirt
had to see the light of day.

@themedochi

Homage to Trees
Marilyn C. Scala

I've been walking a lot lately
as weather warms and
trees stand stately in
their winter skeletons.
I used to think they were
just plain bare in winter
until I got to know them on
long walks and notice the
surprising variety of their limbs.
Some trees spread branches
straight to the sky, while others
reach haphazardly with
unexpected twists and turns,
like a jazz piece,
full of improvisation.

The calendar says spring, but
spring is full of indecision as
snow flutters down.
Purple crocuses are not
intimidated and bravely sit
next to a patch of snow,
promising the new season.
Days pass and under warmer
blue skies, bare branches
leisurely burst into a
kaleidoscope of pink and
white blossoms. Soon
the splendid skeletons
begin to leisurely uncurl
their light green leaves.
Spring is working
it's magic, dabbling
colors everywhere.

Bees buzz around
these early blooms,
and birds chirp, hidden by
the birth of new foliage.
Spring, defining a season
long awaited and vigorously
enjoyed, will soon slide
into summer.

july is wilting
rauren w

wednesday morning crêpes
technicolor roosters
following the leader on the wall
even fake flowers are wilting
on the counter

I am flesh of her flesh
I am bone of her bone
I do not share her freckles
and I wish I wore her nose

july is wilting
march will come
following the leader
I will still be home of her home

@raurenpoetry

My handshake speaks culture
Benidamika Jones Latam

This evening I cooked with my mother,
adding turmeric to almost every dish and I thought,
"how very Indian of us,"
but

when I say I love orange, I meant the orange of a pumpkin,
an apricot, carrots. The orange of safety vests,
a traffic cone; the orange in any thing but not
the orange on my hands.

I sit in class and hide them underneath my thighs,
inside my bag; always searching
for something I purposely forgot.
I curl my fingers around my pen, into a fist of shame
till my handwriting is not my own.

I am ashamed.
Ashamed of people and their thoughts on yellow hands.

Mother always taught me to wash my hands
twice after dinner, but what can I do
when my culture clings to my nails -
waiting to be shown off like a new manicure
to the first person I meet.

This shame has evolved, it is now a shame of touching
food.
When I was in college, I spent a year eating
with a spoon just to avoid orange. Just so
I can tuck my hair behind my ears without any anxiety.
I denied myself the joy
of eating with my hands, just to feel pretty.

But this evening, I cooked with my mother.
I refilled our little turmeric jar and gave it back to her.
I watched her add color to our food and said,
"maybe, just a little more".

@chasxng.auroras

The Language of Home
Helena Kobayashi-Wood

My mother taught me
My mother's tongue
Contorting around the words
She knew so well

When her lips parted
Sound escaping
She could hear home
calling

But I would only complain
My jaw aching
For the words
I could only hold in my palm
Yet could not taste

Now
I cherish the light switch
That language is to me

I feel the tug of the string
That ties me to a place I have never lived in
Does not have my height chart
Etched on the doorframe
Or mundane memories
Tucked into every nook and cranny
And yet
I still call it home

@the.light.of.living

mother's chicken noodle soup
Lixin Tan

my childhood sat in a china bowl
of my mother's chicken *mee sua*,
steaming softly like her temper:
mouthfuls of biting, scalding words;
a mist that both enveloped and avoided
my face, a reluctant hug; warm soup,
a muted apology that secretly blanketed
me at night; noodles like strings of questions,
how are you? can you care for yourself?
will you stay home?

my dreams hid here too. i imagined
stowing away memories of my mother
in checked luggage, living in a new city
where foreign tongues mispronounce
her dish in conversations about home,
renaming it like internet recipes that
carelessly teach about replacements
and substitutes. *you may replace*
your mother with a pinch of salt.

when my childhood ended, the tip
of my tongue continues to burn
occasionally. i never left home and
i still sleep in the mellow fragrance
of soy sauce and sesame oil. i changed
my diet and i don't eat chicken *mee sua*
anymore, but a pot of my mother's cooking
is always firmly planted on our table top,
an open invitation to come home.

@lixin.tan

Seville
Shristi Das

I sit under a greenwood tree, hidden away from the keeps
of a blanched sun,
Sheltered under the shrouds of a hazy March afternoon, I
let my mind skip and run,
I dreamt of sunkissed wheatgrass, black currant orchards
and perfumed raspberry bushes,
I dreamt of You, your dark ombre eyes, your itchy
Christmas sweater and your whiskey induced rushes,
Woke up with a glorious smile,
Do you remember those nights in Seville, when lovers drew
wanton breaths under the crimson moon?
Memories of you are like dazzling mirages in a torrid
desert, breathless to witness but snatched away too soon

@peachteamusings

check your privilege.
Colleen Tubungan

skins don't have to be white to have rights.
skins don't have to be white so you can safely
walk by without a pointed gun aimed at your heart.
skins don't have to be white to wake,
breathe and sleep in no fear.
skins don't have to be white to
have a right to simply live.

@lostandstars

39

dynamite
s.t. tuchin

tempted by new thoughts of her;
fantasies of her touch,
newfound desire for her affection.
the way she could make you feel
and the effortless intensity of your connection,
previously forgotten
but remembered in its absence.
you pine for her presence,
excited at just the thought
of what she can do to you.
to see and laugh with her again
sparked a flame that has since
burned out;
a flame you want so bad to reignite.

but you snuffed that fire,
long ago,
knowing how quickly it could spread.

not the spark of a flame
but a fuse
to a bomb instead.
no affection is worth such dynamite;
the fire burned out -
do not risk lighting the fuse
for just one more night.

@reservoirsummer

All this fruit
Alice Doig

We used to sing
Of strange fruit
Hanging in trees;
Of purpled feet
Dangling down
From black bodies.

Yet decades later
- with these trees cut down -
Their roots
Their fruits
Are pressed to ground;
Are juiced of life
And stigmatised,
Are rallied
Bullied
Sacrificed
As martyrs in this war on life -
These neighbours, mothers, husbands, wives;
These cousins, brothers, sisters lives
Are snatched away
Whilst the white man thrives;

And still
- all this fruit -

dehumanised.

@alicemaypoetry

Vanishing Act
Melissa Anderson

breath on a chilled window pane
fog reaching from its center
expanding outward
daring to take up space
quietly it lingers
begging to be noticed
before it begins to vanish
leaving only a soft trace

@melissal.anderson

on the boil
tb finch

in our nest
daddy cooked the eggs

feeding the flames
then plopping them into
the popping, steaming pan

he'd watch them rattle
in an infinite boil

so when the shell was cracked
they weren't soft inside

@tb.finch

Warmth
Chandrika K

Sunflowers bloom inside my belly,
they root themselves to my favourite yellow dress,
warming my skeletons and I look like summer.
Extremely ripe guavas turn yellow,
raising up ghastly smells in storage sheds,
but straw yellow hay covers them up-
now look for a guava in the haystack.
Yellow is the turmeric my mum puts in milk,
when my throat can't sing and my nose can't breathe-
guess this is wishful thinking,
but they soak the flowers in me with a yellow tinge.
I wait for summers because they bring in the yellows-
mangoes, pineapples and jackfruits.
At 11:11 twice in a day, eating with hands varnished in
golden hues;
Amber coloured honey makes red blood blushing cheeks
but yellowing leaves of giant lonely trees, tell stories of
bloody teeth.
Nevertheless, thank you for wearing your lemon tinted
glasses
and reading the poems in these Bangalore Yellow Pages,
and reminding me that summer is not just a season.
Summer is me.

@moonsrika

traditional chinese parents eat whole fish
Lixin Tan

in an indian restaurant
we sat across lime green tables
jammed into blue floors. we were
the only chinese people, our skin
subtle yellow sheen under fluorescent,
your fingers like chopsticks used
for the first time as they lifted the pages
of the menu. my hands were surer
of themselves, thumbing through the
menu like a book i pretended to read,
a rhythm that concealed your indecision.
i already knew my favourite food,
bhatura, appam, puri, naan,
their names more familiar than the sound
of your tongue shifting vowels,
your polished consonants a cacophony
of insects flying into the electric trap.

you pointed at the picture of a fried fish,
eyes glazed with flour, its mouth gaping
suffocating under the blanket of chilli paste.
my parents eat whole fish and i don't
because i can see the animal. i imagined
dinner with your parents, a steamed fish
glowering at you with marbled eyes,
daring you to prod it with a fork,
but the pale skin around your own eyes
scrunched up as you squeezed them
shut, pursed lips holding back criticism
so it wouldn't lose itself in the clinking
of chopsticks dipping food into soy sauce,
accented like your parents' english.

you ordered *palek paneer* but the picture
of the fried fish never left our minds.
i should have taken you to mcdonalds'.

@lixin.tan

Peace is a Song Illegal to Sing.
Sean Murphy

what will it take to end
violence and discrimination?

well, they say,
"it ain't over
till the fat lady sings."
so what did they do?
they sewed
her mouth shut,
so she'll never sing again.
she's now 90lbs,
on the brink of
starving to death,
begging through muffled sounds
to sing one more song
before her heart
stops beating.

we're running out of time.

@seanfrancismurph

Existential Thoughts On a Tinder Date
Shanai Tanwar

I drop myself
home because

modern dating
is moral less

I am more in
command of
the spread of my legs than
getting a call

back.

there is something
otherworldly
about having somebody
for only
a night

ah! the amnesia
of the ambrosia
in the few hours spent;
a meaningless existence

maybe speed
dating
is the technocratic
solution
to modern
exis-
ten-
tial-
ism

I find you,
a wave of light,

in the white noise of the bar
and forget what
it means to be
suspended in outer space

I find you
you find me
and the combustion
has an
expiry date

@inkbyshanai

- **shaking hands with my own aphantasia.**
g.d. bubb

Here's a list of things I cannot see:

What I want my life to look like in five years.
The menu board at my local Tim Hortons.
When my imaginary therapist softly says
"Picture yourself on a beach somewhere relaxing".
(Beaches aren't relaxing Debroah, sand is evil)
The Canucks getting into playoffs this season.
How I would look if I never had a tattoo addiction.
Bananas, blueberries or strawberries.
The architectural design of the Oslo Opera House.
A smile on my younger self.

@g.d.bubb

Damp socks in an English garden
Flanna Lindsay

I wear my socks
As they grow damp in an English garden.

One filled with the flowers of nostalgia.
Forever a place, a space of mine,
To abscond to in my mind.

Her table built of white, wrought iron.
Its legs, plants, vine-like creepers.
Growing from the earth
As if it had always existed.

I wedge my fingers in the grooves of its floral top,
Tasting peaches and bubbles in the air.

I remove my socks and dance.
With the naked ghosts of forgotten summer parties.

The dewy drops, dressing blades,
Forming pathways in my wake.
They tickle my soul and soles,
Whilst the plumes of cigarette smoke...
Slowly spiral into –

The neighbouring gardens of memories.

@poemblem

A Dragon's Mother.
the medøchï

My mother is a brave woman.
She looked the dragon dead in his eyes,
and didn't falter to bear all and take on
the burden after. At that time I couldn't,
taming him wasn't

even something I could dream of.
I just hoped he would never wake. Another
foolish dream, because letting him free
ended self-torturous ways. So now I bear it all
but, there's no burden. So I'll never be as
strong as that Queen, that's for certain.

@themedochi

49

FREE exPRESSion
Nathan Anton

Being a storyteller at heart,
I got my start
Working as a journalist.
It enabled me to provide a public service.
It gave me purpose.

However, I went from being career-driven and focused
To unemployed and hopeless.

The details can be discussed at a later time,
Because I don't want to taint the vibe of this rhyme.

Long story short,
I was fired for filing a report.

I did what I had to do
When my newsroom fell through.

My worldview was corrupted by the corruption.

I was naive to believe
The press could be free.

Yet, this didn't stop me.
I told the truth independently.

As a result, four public figures had to resign.
Which at the time, I thought was a good sign.

Unfortunately, I was told
My journalism career had met the end of its road.

I thought they were lying.
So I started applying.

Not a single callback in more than three years,
Which is why I inevitably had to switch gears.

Now, I work in IT,
And sometimes struggle with depression and sobriety.

I've tried to take my own life--
Not once or twice, but thrice.

After that last attempt,
Off to rehab I went.

This is not me,
Nor whom I want to be.

I want to belong.
I want to surround myself with people who are passionate
and strong.

I want to live and relate.
I want to co-create.

###

@noahXnight

This is Me
Shristi Das

This is me,
Standing at the doorway, begging him to stay,
Looking away from the mirror in contempt, to ignore my imperfections, just for today

This is me,
Telling myself, again and again, to trust my gut because the instincts always know it all along,
Blotting my charcoal black mascara tears, asking myself, to hold on and be strong

This is me,
Slowly learning to fall in love, with the wrinkles around my eyes, the stretch marks on my thighs, the patches on my skin and the gap between my teeth,
Travelling solo, Learning to play the violin, listening to some "uncool" music, taking up a "dead" language, exposing the mended scars under a healing sheath

This is me,
Ditching away the weight of glitter and all the dazzling stars of a millions galaxies, to spend a night conversing with the Moon,

This is me,
Kicking back, adding some cardamom to my ginger tea, embracing myself and all the conditions that apply,
dancing the night away to my own graceful heart's tune

@peachteamusings

Anyutha Norin Salim

Growing up, I had one best friend. Ever since I'd turned fifteen, she'd showed up. Persistent. Always, uninvited. On the darkest mornings and brightest nights, she sat beside me, always in a yellow pinafore. When she tried to hold my hands, I pinched her wrists. I'd be laughing with my sister, or murmuring my favorite song, or softly nursing a blue hydrangea, when she'd sneak up from behind. Envelope me. Fondly. One day, I decided to lock her up in a wooden almirah in the attic. This had to be it, I'd decided. Only, she came back manifold, knocking down my walls. I tried to run, hide or even make new friends. She shut the door on their face, and latched it tight. Years had passed before I finally asked her her name. On that warm summer evening, I exhaled snowflakes. I held her hand, and sat with her for hours. She traced my palms in circles of two before she finally let go. Today, she's not my only friend, but always a dear one.

-on a dear friend named Sorrow

@anyuthanorin.writes

A Drinker with a Writing Problem
James Goggin

I typed three poems last night
But could only remember
Writing the first one. The last two
Were born from brainless fingers.

I read the two blackout babies
And laughed because they weren't very good
But I also like them better
Than a lot of my others.

I've had a few blackouts
Where the next day I woke up
Somewhere I shouldn't be
With a displeased cop or a strange woman
Looming over my half-dead body.

Waking up on my couch
With two bad poems seems like progress
To me.

@barfly_poetry

vacant lots
Kim Backalenick Escobar

she was lost in a vacant lot/reading comic
books/to find meaning in life/she crawled
inside empty cans of cat food/looking for
scraps and the taste of love/she'd seen
her future years before/and collected
shopping carts and thrown out food/like
she was practicing/but her lipstick was
still cherry red/and on alternate days/
mango tango/and she was more than she'd
have you believe/a queen/always high on
pepsi and life/and the belief that
strangers could be friends/she hid
struggles in crumbled newspapers and
old bread/and folded herself into a
paper airplane to dive into dumpsters
to find vestiges of herself/she'd cast
off in another lifetime/

@edgeofpoetry

Shadow Dancer
Joanne F. Blake

To never see your smile again.
or smell the aroma of your scented skin
To imagine that you're near me.
but it's only a fantasy
To call and there's no answer,
I can't bear the thought of losing you
Awaken my Shadow Dancer

@joannethepoetess

mom mom

rauren w

a handful of memories:
a garden
a tree swing
a gap peeking from between boards in the fence
a soft afternoon
crowning a holly bush with little treasures
a small television
Star Trek
a perm and a comb and a no
a sleepover and unbrushed teeth
pudding cups
and a fireplace

four hallmark cards
five words
(I will always love you)
two x's
two o's

but it's hard to picture you.

@raurenpoetry

Daily Miracles
James Goggin

Perhaps to God
The spinning of planets
And the burning of stars
Is as mundane as our trip
To the grocery store and cleaning
The ring from the bathtub.

Perhaps to God
There's nothing all that special
To the infinity of Time
Or the expanse of the Universe
And They are flipping through Galaxies
Like we browse Netflix for hours.

I can't say for certain
But I have a strong feeling
That God only finds one thing
Profound. How our fearful little species
Can still manage to be kind. Perhaps we
Are more impressive than stars
When we stretch out
Our hand.

@barfly_poetry

Softball in Rampart, AK
Camden Michael Jones

The locals invite us for an evening game;
the town has 27 residents
and most worked today.

The Rampart team comes slowly,
dressed in waders and mitts in hand,
riding quads with beer coolers
in back.

They take the field first,
arrayed against a forested
backdrop and smoking,
all of them smoking
drinking running running
running as the softball skips
across the ground like so many
days flown by too quickly.

We mark ten runs and swap,
taking places with 11 pm shadows
following us.

The never-setting sun
plays with our hair
as one hand might
play with the wind while driving,
that is, all fingers;
our own are spread between leather
webs and dusty stitches;
the ash on our hands
settles into our palm lines;
and we play deep into the night
on a gravel airstrip overlooking
the Alaskan interior.

@camden.m.jones

Bread Crumbs
Desirée Heltzel-Baylin

i wonder if things will change
or if they'll stay the same
will people leave legacies
and bread crumb trails to walk
for children to find their way
did i do enough for my family
or did i somehow lose my way
these are things i ask myself
when i awake every single day

@baylinwriting

Dustlight
Rosslyn Chay

Cedar brown and cream twists,
running six feet by four, the marker
of the living hall, elevating
this transient abode to a home.

A dimension into indolence,
an alluring offer for an afternoon delight.

Settle into the twin sofa,
let your soles caress the twisted fibers,
and marvel at the holy sight—
motes afloat, scintillating
in the stream of light.

@voicesofyun

The colour of falling
Akshata Lanjekar

The first time you see it,
falling appears a warm maroon.
Like the bench you stubbed your toe on
or the dried blood on your knee
from when you slipped off the slide in the park.
The first time you meet falling,
it is always in a literal fall.
You meet it suspended mid air,
and as the world slows down
all you can think of is that this is the worst
falling will ever hurt.
Maroon falling is a friend to bandages
and the smell of dettol and off days from school.
Maroon falling is the security of your mother's soup
and your father's worried glances.

When you meet falling again it looks blue.
Like the clear sky in spring and
the ocean waves kissing your feet
as you stand holding hands with
the boy of your dreams,
falling in love. They call it falling in love
because once you dive in, you don't get to come up for air.
So you fill your lungs
for a lifetime of diving, in him.
Blue falling makes you feel like your favourite song, dew
sitting on huge lotus leaves,
and swarms of dragonflies in your sky whispering that rain
is on its way.
Your gut always flutters
and your heart is lighter than cotton candy.
Blue falling is adventure of first kisses and pride of
anniversaries.

The next time you stumble across falling,
it is blacker than the blackest black you've ever seen and
you almost don't know its there until

you start falling into the abyss.
It comes as sudden as rain clouds in Mumbai
and takes you down the gutters
into the underworld.
Black falling makes you ride the ferris wheel
with your demons while the world watches on
as they do an otter in an aquarium
Black falling is the pain of bones not yet broken
and the despair of dreams not yet crushed.

And
just as you start believing you live in a round world
you will meet falling again around a corner.
It will creep up on you like the sun creeps up on the night
and you will see,
it shines bright yellow, and it reminds you
of sunflowers and daffodils
and the colour of the dress you bought
with your first paycheck.
Yellow falling would catch you unaware
like a wisp of sweet fragrant lilies from
the neighbor's garden, as you
fall for yourself this time.
You will look at yourself in the mirror at the golden hour
and see flowers dripping from your skin
and exclaim what a blessing it is
to have woken up that day!
Yellow falling is the comfort of finding home
in yourself and peace of knowing
what falling truly feels like.

@worldinherwords

I Look for Myself
Talina Dimond

I look for myself in the oddest of places
Like old, run-down diners
And the back roads of hell
Or at 4 am, in an acquaintance's stairwell

Standing around neon-lit alleyways
With dumpsters and cigarette butts
Finding peace when I feel messy
After obnoxiously spilling my guts

The empty airport terminal
Knows me so well
As does the vacant park
Where the air of my childhood dwells

The wide desert-scape
Has heard me curse and cry
The bathroom of the Ace Hotel
Has watched me retch and say permanent goodbyes

I've left pieces of myself
In so many places
But I've felt like it's them
That have left the most meaningful traces

@the_passionate_verse

Barflies
John Rock

Locals with stories
 to tell
   (mostly sad)
Carpet blushes
neglected, bored and
 caught unawares.
Incomplete crosswords
a brief respite as legitimate
   thoughts attempt
       breaching of doors
(Bad for business).

Strict moral dress code
    hoodwinks yet again
as does a bogus racing tip
from nondescript, sweaty man.
The landlord rubs
     his hands together
either for warmth or
        punctuation
as he prays for rain
(good for business).

@johnrockpoet

to die from virus, to die from hunger.
Colleen Tubungan

i scrape my bones to pay monthly bills
with a pocket full of half minimum wage.
all i need is an eye of pity to get the best deals;
the left over ones thrown to a bin of waste.
i think the news reported virus as deadly
but i can't hear a single thing from my
children's scream, "i am hungry!"
since then, schools say you need the
internet and laptop screens to own
so i wash more sheets until morning
with blunted hands alone to buy my son
an off-brand touchscreen phone.
i live to sweat tears to live in loans
so maybe this time, you'll quit saying,
"it's not that hard to stay at home."

@lostandstars

06 24 20
J.R. Taylor

Nesting birds
pick up the shedded hair
brushed from the dogs

"FUCKING DEPENDENT SOCIALIST!
GET A GODDAMN JOB!'

they fly away
into palaces we'll never know

"FUCKING SCUM!
LEECHING OFF THE SYSTEM!"

cut the tree down
bring us all down

@j.r.taylor_writes

Oh - lief klein nachtegaal
Kimberley Chung

As curtains draw the night
starlings take flight,
up, up - they go,
wings flapping, flapping
into a flock of murmuration.

At that time,
a sweet wee nightingale
whistles and whispers
folktales and fables,
secrets of the nature
in the dead of the night.

Oh - lief klein nachtegaal,
your crystalline voice
makes ripples in the wind,
as you lull the restless
back to sleep,
back to sleep.

@dearchinagirl

Café

James McNinch

Sipping my peppermint tea
Smelling, as peppermints do,
Of a cover up.
A masked scent.
A concealed truth.

Isn't it strange how you can
Sit in a café amongst others
Yet still be absolutely alone?
Or step into a crowd
And see nobody?

Goodness, I've waited a
Long time
For my sausage roll
(Vegan, of course).
Ah! Here it is!

Where was I?
Yes.
Isolation.

Of course, my thoughts isolate me
My emotions, my feelings.
My desire to love
Who I want to love
And not the woman
Society thinks is right.

Perhaps the peppermint tea
Is drowning out my inner voice?
Or perhaps not.
I'll never really know.

So it sit back,
Have another sip of tea
(Now moderately lukewarm),
And smile.

The peppermint masks me perfectly.

@poems_by_a_musician

diversity leash
Lea Abboud

we love diversity,
they said,
as they put a leash
on who constituted
that diversity.

@labboudx

Shadow
In The Ether

These jobs get fucking tedious
but they pay well

Coming to the bar after has become ritual
I've discovered I prefer Rye to Bourbon

Another woman will approach

Something about my eyes or lips

She will serve a purpose tonight

Her elegant lies
Messianic complex

It's always the broken ones
that are going to save me

I was born with Adermatoglyphia
I have no fingerprints

The perfect criminal

I never understood why my father
would continuously break my nose
when I was a teenager

At age 19
he took a tire iron to my teeth
so I would have a mouthful of dentures
In case anything went wrong
I would never be identified

I will always be a shadow

He said I would understand
when the family business was mine

He was right
He was always right

Before they burned his body
he prepared me for the dark world
that would make me wealthy

I'm not into redheads
but it's last call
plus she only lives 2 blocks away
I have to double-check my passport
to see who I am tonight

Eric Mitchell
Lafayette, IN

Close enough to Chicago without being Chicago
Not that it matters
She is too drunk to remember anything
I slip out as soon as she falls asleep

Back to the grind

2 weeks later...

There were no bars after this job

Dry county
Tennessee State Senator
with an affinity for kiddie porn

I found a diner
endless coffee
decent eggs
great apple pie

I remember the last thing this prick said to me
before I slammed the two screwdrivers
into each temple

"You don't know how important I am!
I know powerful people!
They will come for you!"

I hear this kind of shit all the time
A dying man's last act of bravado

I'm the one they send

The only one

Because
I was never born
so I can never die

@in_the_ether_poetry

United
Tanya Vanpraseuth

We will advocate for equality
For a change
A new sight
We won't cower to injustice
We won't stop our fight

We won't let our differences separate us
Or believe that we are divided
Just imagine all that we can do,
Once we are all UNITED.

@tanya.van

house tour
Jaden Ogwayo

splintered oak shards and rusted nails mosaic a path to the estate—mind your step. under the wood; lava-like quicksand. she is picky. her golden grains choose who floats and sinks. previous astray tenants slipped through the sand like stray cats into sewers. in her warm smother, quicksand provides shelter from life's rain. cracked windows provide broken rays of light to trickle through the home. overgrown ivy vines cascade down the home's facade; further protection from the outside world. a slanted tile roof frames the home; a head of terracotta hair. the mahogany doorbell rings! embrace the echoes of masked pain and muffled screams—accompanied by a robotically strummed harp. crawl on your knees like an infant to fit under the door and be careful of the sharp edges. the door is broken but still permeable. its razor-like frame is full of splinters to deter visitors. this house was once one of many rooms but the previous owner saw fit to convert to open living. faint floral scents waft through this space to rejuvenate a wavering mind. as lavender calms, rose lulls. embrace the power of such smells. they distract the olfactory from the cobwebbed curtains. to your left, this ivory wall was once a kitchen. caress the plaster. take in the aromas of culture. dulled by a lick of fresh alabaster, the house cries out not to be forgotten. legally, we're required to inform buyers of previous deceased owners. boredom kills. melancholy; life's torture. add a plant! paint a wall! breathe life in here. here are the keys.

@jadenwrites

she still writes
Colleen Tubungan

she still writes with sacred flaws in and out of places
and he's never known a pair of eyes so genuine
the ones that makes you believe that
sunflowers still grow in darkness

@lostandstars

HONESTLY WHY
Claire Allen

it keeps raining despite
the clouds in your eyes
the kind of fog that can't be
blown away with tender sighs
i'll wait in the car
windows up until
you come slinking back
plastic bag held aloft like a solo cup
no one told me when the party
started so I showed up
underfed and badly dressed
the motel down the street
has a vacancy if I'm
looking for a bad place to die
honestly why

@paper_worlds

armistice
s.t. tuchin

blasting through the hollow walls
of my gently crumbling tower of existence,
the cannonballs of your dismay
pummeling my stone.
keeping white flags
neatly folded,
writing on the wall
the need to stand strong.

months of holding off
this assault,
taking the hits and
holding fire,
these walls are starting to
        collapse.
your kingdom against my lonely,
        lowly castle,
demanding my surrender.
as the doorways collapse behind me,
i make my way to
        the docks
and raise my flag.
like a sinking, flaming vessel
i send my parting gift -
a closing ceremony,
a long-sought armistice.

@reservoirsummer

Splitting the kids for tax season
Arthur Willhelm

I broke down somewhere
Along the parkway
Life gets heavy like
That sometimes
On the lonely drive
After taking my children
Home
Two days a week
I get them two fucking
days a week
There are nights that
I get sick to my stomach
Because I miss them
And a phone call
Isn't enough
The ex-wife became
A two headed snake
Money became
an obsession
The children became
a tool
And slowly I felt more
and more hollow
They are my blood
Goddamnit
Every day that I'm
not with them
Is another day of their
Lives that I lose
The guilt consumes
Me and it feels like
The earth could
Swallow me whole
I broke down somewhere
Along the parkway
Life gets heavy like
That sometimes.

@arthurjwillhelmpoetry

Fallen Leaves
Avalone Rae

I like to paint trees from fallen leaves,
Parched and matted,
These leaves once a part of the tree,
Now decorates the walking ground.

These leaves, cut off but free,
Revel in giving, down to earth,
Enriched and enriching,
This soil they all came from.

Because fallen leaves,
Even if stamped upon,
Gently nurturing,
To the tree that shed them once,
Because fallen leaves,
A home to the homeless,
Yet you sweep them away,
With the trash.

@avalone.rae

coffee cuddles
Prynne Argo

caffeine swirls embraces me
early in the morning autumn days
that warmth I cherish the most.

@prynne.poetry

the tiny quiet killing
Nik Knoppová

he's smoking outside a highway motel we're mid nowhere
south of somewhere soaked in saving

only because it aged well + far away + I wonder if she
knows
about the smell on his collar it's treacherous

I don't wonder if she knows everything else he lives in
secret
such a red blooded monument that to even look would
make a past

a present is delicate under fingertips pressing into live
human skin – no
I'm nine + know how to worry about secondhand smoke

how to close my eyes when it threatens to cloud them
+ it's what I'll do like a prayer

the tiny quiet seeping between the alarm yellow lines
in the pavement.

@nk_poet

Lachrymose
Sam Drury

I will boil your wartime souvenirs to extract drugs for
much needed peacetime. You left me cold and curious
yet you're the one who weeps into the handkerchief.
We're always covered by thunder and get cut by the
lightning shard, it was okay for a time but now the
wounds created just seep into my prison food you made.

Never could an ocean hold me to its shore, you know but
now all that seems to happen is a routine crash down,
pull back and repeat. I remember the days of standing
calm with all its motion with all the movement of its
flow, never even imagined the notion of anything less
but like a rabbit out of a hat pulled by claws that yours
have a uncanny resemblance to.

I feel useless when I have to face alone the legion of
walls you've surrounded me with. If I could only slip
away and ride out the wave you've created.
I'm just not sure I can take us forward now,
I don't think I know how.

@samdrurypoem

muscle memory
Sophie Powell

falling, but it's a
slow fall

a fall with ropey arms
and sweet, fresh breath, and
when both brush flesh
it's new

it's a fall which slowdances
with me,
and then with you
and when we've traced
eachother's footsteps
my muscle memory
can't look back.

gushing,
only for -
always for you
gushing a waterfall
to fund growing blue

gushing, blood rushing when
a private smile is cracked,
gushing certain words
at first, a fancy
now a fact

but dry waters
and bittersweet
pay rent, then reproduce
plaguing our softest silences,
they curse us for our youth.

when it's sense is dulled
by homely soil,
my muscle memory forgets steps

but eye contact breaks anchors,
and your smile does not forget.

slowdancing
is escapism
and astral
and insane
today, we claim
a pair of daylight hours
tomorrow, we do the same

and when I wake,
the light hasn't had chance
to cross the blue
but I endure the time difference
and then,
again,
I fall for you

@decaffeinatedpoetry

Today is a Good Day
Zohra Nizami

Yesterday was all blue with specks of grey
with the smell of a rainy day,
not rain that washes dirt away but a drizzle
that wets things and makes them stick;
yesterday was not a good day.
But today there is a sparrow on my window sill
singing a greeting to the breeze
making a pretty blanket with fallen leaves
for the ground that is peering at the sky
so hopefully, and somewhere someone
is humming a tune tenderly like they want today
to taste of sweetness;
I feel warmth growing inside me —
me a fireplace in an abandoned home.

@z.n.writes

Beer Garden
Samantha McGowan

Sticky tabletops littered with half empty glass
grass scattered with faded umbrellas
emblazoned with brands of beer and tonic
we were high on summer and late nights
but the light still hung in the sky past 9pm
I remember sitting on a wall with the others
a collection of scraped knees and bruised shins
dangling off the ground as the sound of laughter
filtered through the open windows
someone's father would exit a smoke-filled doorway
with an armful of treats
just a normal Saturday night
and it never occurred to us to mind
sipping on Panda Pop and munching on crisps
we were the orphans of The Fox & Hound

@daisy.press.poetry

The Carrying Pole
Lucia Irvine

A flurry of garden rakes welded to chimneys,
Stand proud in their efforts to gather the stillness of a day,
The inconsequential nature of the day as it hangs in the air,
Like the strewn denim jacket that returned to the banister
as quickly as it was removed,
The rakes are massaged by the crow's feet,
As it two steps to the soft sound of a distant paddling pool,
And to the delights of children being hosed down by their
mother,
Who moves in autopilot and wears a vacant look in her
eyes,
Her own crow's feet lie in thick streaks and her
ineliminable consciousness visible,
As it hangs on her shoulders like a carrying pole,
One bucket overflowing,
The other half-empty as she teeters,
Struggling to bear the load.
The frothy milk of lifelong guilt for the choices she made
that led her here,
Beneath the insignificance of a blue sky,
And below the birds she stands above in the food chain.
The water she douses her children in,
A lifeline she can't quite grasp,
Unless she pacifies those hindering thoughts that swell in
the buckets
Or simply sets them down,
Or drinks them up.

@badgirlwrites

81

Shivers
Ruth Isabella Peters

I lay in the grass.
Right where you laid.
The weather is holding on to the last traces of Summer,
while Winter awaits at the gates.
A cold wind surrounds me. The feeling so intense, it makes
the hair on my body rise.
I pray, that the clouds make way for the sun.
I pray, God gives me one more day of Summer.
One more day of light and laughter.
As the clouds fade, I warm up. My heart melts and I
remember his voice.
His deep voice reverberating through me.

And I shiver.
I shiver like I used to.

@ruthisabellaa

celestial millennial
Ivy K. Stone

i dream in stars
weaving in and out of planets
meteors that invade
nightmares and wake me from a restless
slumber
i am naive
to think we are alone in the galaxy
to be unafraid
of a cosmic being that could
materialize—a comet, a piece of a planet—
and destroy the clouds
i fly so high on.

@traces.of.ivy

Selfhood
Liliana Aleman

on my own
by myself in the hourly hades
i am here again

when peace is now movement and miles seem to misgive
there came a minute during those stages of age
where organically i found places to live
and people who dwell homes
that no reason lied to call permanence onto deliverance

but it comes and drains and turns on it's side
so it seems just another wednesday afternoon

that while life was here and i was there
somewhere amongst the branches fall
my wound stopped its bleed

because as i've run from the pressure without anywhere as
to go
my heart started to beat
my spirit started to release
and i started to heal

no time of mine had been spent glancing around
to notice the tree house of selfhood subconsciously
link who i was to who i am now

so like this i want to thank every departure or extremity
that adverted my directions to be led away
as this whole offset prepared me to uncover unfolding
space
in sanctions i always thought to ignore
and despite this place being welcoming before,
the feeling has all well changed

i lastly now see that this time i arrive home to be made in
me

@lilianaas_

Alamort
Prena Subba

you wouldn't realize until
all the stars in your bones 'explode'
and haunt you with my mortal remains.
because I am pathetically made up of
bottled oceans, roaring blizzards,
cracked vases and an empty heart,
all just the way you were built before
until you got lost and never came back.
and see how beautifully I live
and achingly lie that I am nothing
but a mere specter of haunted hopes
and long gone heart beats.

@prena.poetry

A complaint from a Rose
Afreeca Daniel

I went to the garden alone.
While the droplets were still coating the Roses
Where the crown of thorns were beheaded
By the bloody red queen
To paint color to a throne
A Jester's preposition.
The Euphorbia milii reached out to me
A small complaint she wished to make.
She talked about her flowers.
Fragile things her branches upheld
For admiration and plucking merit
She told me about an unfair order
Of knights and kings
Horsemen and queens.
About when her roses have been taken away
She's rarely ever seen.
About how others only saw her top
While the way up was cursed to wear the veils.
She shed dews of tyranny
That fell on a pack of cards
Her life as a Jack that nobody
Celebrated.
As branches of heros with repulsive
Thorns until the next bloom.
She thanked me for the ear but before I turn to leave,
I told her we were somewhat kinda like her
She said she knew.
And I wondered who else, not like men, knew too.

@freekah_mali

85

a garden rose
Shashwat Indeevar

and quite so soon
the same red rose
that took a season
to fully bloom
wilts when the wind
bellows and blows
rain plays its part
showers down hard
taking proud petals
and lush leaves apart
its sweet scent fades
in the mild petrichor
nothing of it remains
except all its thorns

@brownbeansauce
@shashwatindeevar

Insanity crawling in
Simon E. Northcott

Hours stretched like chewingums,
But tasteless after weeks
In the mouth. I lay
Flat on the floor, horizontal,
Eyes shut, like a dropped pencil
With the tip blunt or maybe
Like a wannabe corpse.
Looking for a different perspective,
Watching the world
From a strange angle:
The light sticks out like a flower
From the ceiling and your eyebrows
Are now the mustache
Above your mouthless forehead.
There is a sort of insanity
Crawling on my tongue
While I laugh madly.
This chewing will choke me
But for now I fear more the time
When these hours will shrink again
Like spinach in a pan.
We won't have time then
To look at the world
With marvelled eyes.

@simone.northcott

Paradigm Shift.
Sean Murphy

someday
you'll have a taste
of your own
tear-gas tiramisu
on a plate
made out of
the bullets
you fired into
the defenseless backs
of innocent people,
who only ever dreamed
of living a life
as peaceful and privileged
as yours.
I hope merely the sounds
of their names
haunt you for not only
this lifetime,
but every lifetime you
undeservedly live.
just as their deaths
were broadcasted to
a nation on two different sides
of a resentful smoke grenade,
so will your comeuppance be.
get ready, assholes.
it's coming.
the dream you've been living
by taking it from those
you keep beneath your boot
is coming to an end.

@seanfrancismurphs

Jerky
Camden Michael Jones

In Queensland, AU
At a convenience store
three kilometres
from our apartment,
we bought a pack
of emu jerky
for the experience.

Spongy, the flesh
of that bird stuck
between our teeth
        it was probably chicken
but our tongues believed
in exotic flavors.

After,
a bus took us
to a wildlife preserve
and our hands
found kangaroo
fur and avian cages.
An emu,
all dinosaur skin
and feathers
        like an overstuffed
hen,
stood before me
as though it could smell
itself in my pores,
and gracefully
wrapped its neck
around my shoulders.
It stood there,
still,
body warm and musty.

@camden.m.jones

89

the closet
Ava Silverman

I sat there in my closet,
with all my clothes,
wondering whether time
would pause to tell me
how long I'd been inside.

//

I'm cleaning my closet,
donating clothes,
stepping out of spaces
I've come to outgrow.

I'm choosing to be heard
instead of trying to stay hidden,
never shrinking back to fit
the small places I have been in.

@make_the_flowers_grow

better days are coming
Vaishaali Saxena

it's been long
since i left my room, or even my bed
since i brushed my hair, roots to tips
since i wore a smile, reaching the eyes;
been long, so long
since the skies have been grey,
the nights, harsh,
and my days, gloomy.

but now, no more;
now i stand and move,
i dress up and groove,
with faith and hope;

for the dawn's near, almost here;
for now, better days are coming
and i must welcome them, with open heart and hands;

i must let them.

@wordsbyv.s

Sadgi Chandra

My lungs are still filled with water
I swallowed when I jumped in the sea
to save your sinking dreams,

These fingers have calluses from
when you gripped them tighter
every time you shove me farther,

My knees are bloody, and bruised and
weak, because you like it when I'm nothing
but a figurine in your lodging,

And can you see my ribs? missing
from my chest because I burned them for you
on a cold night as your nails were blue,

It has been years since I washed you off
but still I'm looking to replace my parts
you left scarred when you ripped out my heart.

@chaosinline

A Curious Sensation
Robert Dominick

the corridor
softly lit and carpeted
behind one of the doors comes laughter
a man's
a woman's
I know where I am
I stand still
my head feels curiously light
weight has been removed
strolling, leaning
mingled with them

@realrobdompoetry

An ode to no one in particular
M.F. Reynoso

I know I have to learn to bend before I break, but I have
listened to the songs and read all the poems describing just
how breathtaking it is to fall apart, how incredibly
beautiful it is not to know how to pull yourself together.
It's not like I'm enamoured with falling down, yet there's
something sweet in going back to the places you know
best, like going home after a long day of work and tucking
yourself tight on warm blankets.

You know I've always wanted to taste like wine and sharp
glass, and you like the girls you can build like legos in your
backyard. Maybe my breaking is not enough to convince
you I'm worth your time, still I kind of like the way it feels
to know I'm giving everything I can until there's nothing
else to give. Until the only thing remaining are the tears
and the heartbreak.

I don't think I love you so much as I love the way I shatter
at your fingertips. Heaven could compose symphonies with
the sound of my chest caving at your goodbyes. Not even
the angels can match my crying at midnight.

So even if you go, I thank you.
For the love
For the loss
For the disaster
For fueling my addiction
For giving me a reason to stay broken
'Cause I'm not myself when I'm whole.
(Now leave me to wallow in my misery.)

@enmictlan

94

Leah Fricke

Kleptomaniac;
I steal
heaviness
from the hands
of others.
I hide away
hurts
I was never meant
to hold.

@when.sunshine.rains

Sunny Love
Ruby Ann Robles

poured chamomile tea in a cup
and took a sliced of cinnamon roll
berries tasted good this time
watching bumblebees alight on daisies
cool weather and feet hid in the sand
bright sun got me tanned
cotton fabric you wore with a familiar smell
water splash and hazy clouds
memories we collected and laughs about
sunny day i wished never to end
warm touch as we hold
and good music that never gets old

@poetry.of.ann

Little girl on the swing under the mango tree
Jeryanne Jane Patayon-Fernandes

Little girl
on the swing under the mango tree
if you can hear me
hear me

You are not alone
here I am a shadow
whispering to you
embracing you

Dont be cold
look at your hands
you carry the stars in your palms
warm and bright

You are safe
the trees protect you
and the rain is your friend
and you your have your words to shield you

Dont guard your heart
your heart is your power
the love you can give and what you're capable to receive
will lead you where you want to be

You are worthy
of all the things coming your way
and you will enjoy the challenges in between your wins
I can see through your eyes

Dont cry in silence
Your cries are a song
and just as much as the world deserves to see your smile
it needs your glorious tears too

You are strong
and brave because you allow yourself to feel

It takes courage to see through life
and let the emotions flow

Little girl
the thoughts you have of being a cloud
you already are
you are free

Little girl on the swing under the mango tree
look at me
I am you
You turned out just fine and even more

@rxewrites

I will fly
Wang Di

I am done,
done,
hosting a pity party
for myself,
cutting my wings off
by magnifying my obstructions.

-I will fly.

@iamwangdiinsta

THERE'S A REASON THELMA AND LOUISE HAD TO DIE IN THE END
Toni H. QSO

I'm only capable of falling completely and mercilessly in love with shitty places.

In my dreams, I can drive.
We're hurling ourselves down the motorway like rain - but its a highway and we're in a 1970s escapism movie where we die at the end
but we love each other so much
It doesn't matter and everyone misunderstands the point.
They see our death as something powerful when really it's demonstrating what should happen to people like us in the eyes of people like them -
And it's just something that happens.

I want my feet on the dash and chewing gum and wind in my hair. I want freedom like in american cinema.
I want to be myself - unlike in american cinema. I want open skies and long roads.
Maybe, in my dreams, I'm the driver because "driver picks the music" and I want to soundtrack whatever happens to us between now and death.

It's just us and our anxious glances in the wing mirror, the rear view mirror, the indistinct voice booming out the dashboard speakers of a post-derby-day football call-in.
I never liked sports but I liked the passion in their voice.
It made me feel a bit less ridiculous in my feelings.
FM radio is a window and its nice to be reminded that the outside world exists and that its beautiful sometimes.

I miss people, I miss how they can fill me up with love or fuck me up like a derelict building. I miss feeling romance and fingers tumbling through my hair; I miss open roads and headaches and bruises from the night before -
But its okay because we're headed somewhere thats supposed to be new, and something new could meet us

there -
And I don't have to live in the house in my head any more,
with thoughts that hurt me, plugged in with a million
wires like a broadcasting server.

We're moving, continiously.
If I could close my eyes, we could go anywhere - on the lam
in my mind into our next life.

@quasistellarobject

Loneliness
Emmy White

Silence takes my coat
And, with hands at my throat,
He welcomes me home.

@poeticallyordinary

An Ode to Arthur Dent's Confusion
Camden Michael Jones

I, too, know the word "Yellow"
floating in gray matter
but I don't have the science
to build robots
with synthetic depression
or how to cope
with thumbs
that never learned
to aim for space
        (are there statistical
        handicaps
        for bad interstellar
        hitchhikers
        like there is in golf)

Is there an encyclopedia
entry for the way
dawn smells on dewy mornings
while lying in a field
outside a pub?
or the thoughts
of sky-bound whales?

I listen to the songs
of this tumbled sea
that is the ground
beneath my back,
and stare at holes
poked in the canvas
above, feeling
for the page edges
of a book
I have yet to write,
feeling for words
that hang the way bricks don't.

What I mean to say,
is I could go for a pint
or three at lunchtime.

@camden.m.jones

Notes on the Bird Gathering at Thomaston Park
Britt Trachtenberg

Overhead, the birds sing in the oak tree
about the children who chase each other and
scream, stepping on grass blades
that do not fry in the sun's eyes.

The cardinal brings up the puffy white line that an airplane left
in the sky, how it looks like it's shrinking
slowly if they squint and hold their breath.
The other birds nod, they say they agree.

The small blue bird talks about the little boy
who rides his bike in circles until he's dizzy,
until he falls to the ground. The other birds laugh,
but to the boy, it's just a chorus of songs.

The warbler brings up the sun,
how it hangs low in the sky, threatening to fall.
He asks if the sun will return tomorrow, and it interjects
with I will.

The cardinal adjourns the meeting, and
all the birds fly away, knowing that this all will happen
another day.

@britt.trachtenberg

Yin and Yang
Akshata Lanjekar

Two people live
in the house of me.
Nice guy smells of the sea,
cooks for pleasure
and buys balloons from kids at traffic signals.
The scamp is a narcissist who
reads philosophy to one up conversations
and loves saying love is dead
while romanticizing suffering
in the name of art.

I sometimes want to kick
the scamp out, and give Nice guy
more room to get comfortable
and achieve his realistic
dreams. A house, a car, a family,
while the scamp learns how to
play the ukulele and walks the streets
drawing portraits of tourists. No matter
how hard I try
I can not fathom the chaos,
the massive glitch
that causes these two to
coexist in me. Afterall
how can I have two extremes
at my heart?
How am I both,
Mountain and beach?

But then I see them everyday,
being the spring to each others winters.
Like those unexplainable friendships
of the wild, they
stick together and every evening at 5,
one brings pockets of day, and
other brings handfuls of night,
together they bask

in the twilight of their kinship
and smile in the knowledge that
there's a little bit of scamp
in nice guy
and a little bit of nice guy
in scamp.

@worldinherwords

seaside eyes
Tala Woods

the air lingers with sea salt and things i wish i had said
i'll always remember the day we met
blue paint on both me
and my head

you walked in, lightbulb
in hand and looking straight ahead -
but you stopped and looked at me

and that was the first time
i saw eyes that were
the same colour
as the sea

@talawrites

Nightshade
Mary Anne Massaro

Nightshade in bloom
On a snippet of lace
Guarding her room
Protecting her space

A pocket garden
On the window sill
Will there be a pardon
For the heartbreaker's kill?

@pixandpoems

Outside and Hazy
Max Larkin

On this ambient dry rock.

I am overly sensitive,
Short of breath, I ache.
Everything that touches me,
does so with an intention to harm.
Scratching failures reside beside me,
screwing ailments into my mind.
Barefoot, I breathe in hope,
as if I'm gasping for it.

The bird whispers its melody,
in this brown and green patch.
An ant climbs the everest of my ankle,
to heights it has never seen.
The flies are doing some reconnaissance,
not one has landed on me yet.
It's as if they know,
I wouldn't be able to bear it.

@conquestwriting

Eugénie Lodier

i first felt the tangy taste of reality
in odd worlds made up by people long dead already

what does that say about what's real?
what does that say about me?

all i know is
there are butterflies and sparkles
in other places than gardens and starry nights

the page will always be where i start looking first

@jamieswrites

Nicole Olmos

Wipe off aphid, underbelly leaf leap to next and loaf there
seeming seam less, more so multiply and re-apply to
morrow. They seem innocent sat sin transparent, eat up
leaf and nectar under nose, tickle squish clock time to wipe
up watching play black grass grow also in revolt and grow
through in Nemesia sun surprise and see it peeking shy in
need of re-pot. Turn down night, callous crack open like
floral unfurl in watch me leather dry taking sweet time to
take from now yes precious. Precious and grateful to look
down and you always here next to next down to wipe up
sink pink colour wheel pick up, bugging you wash sponge
fry, sarn which, making plans for other times little busy
business remnant remedy and brand new box. Oh how in
quack meant luck in hand me down consciousness in
tween those of furlough fly by further and worry only little
less of little mint morrow tangle tinge perhaps on tongue,
feeling slightly tight to alliterate much, try the other
tongue a lopsided grin reversible, with the reminder to sit
upright and keep flowering.

@pastpoetry_

Legacy of An Only Child
Harriet Shenkman

Legacy of An Only Child

I used to watch Ozzie and Harriet

The family sat around a dining table
Harriet served meals off white china,
wore a ruffled apron and a string of pearls.
They may have had a dog named Ruff.

The three of you

sat around our oval dining table.
I never wore an apron
but we did have a border collie mix
who only herded squirrels.

At my demise

don't expect pearls or bone china,
not even a leather bible,
but to you, and you and you,
I bequeath two siblings each.

You can quibble over

Who is the most challenging ?
The child who is totally annoying ?
The sibling likely to steal the spotlight ?

@h.s.poetess

Aurora of Dawn
Kathryn Kluttz

the fresh sting of daybreak
burns my milky flesh til I am blushed red
from the blazing sun overhead
for what can I do
when my only reprieve from the cold arms of night
is to boil myself under a fiery sky
fixated on the raging flames
as they kiss my skin
and brush my mortality with its angry light so bright
I am recklessly aware of my impending ephemerality
as one last time I embark outside
into the gleaming rays of fire.

@hailspoetry

Sadgi Chandra

I'm made up from the silence
of women who came and went
before me,
so it's only fair that
I'll scream,
there is a rage in me, a soft
madness roaring,
I'm here because
they suffered bravely,
now it's only fair that
I do everything to make sure
no one else does
after me.

@chaosinline

Pocket full of gemstones
Stephanie Robertson

With a pocket full of gemstones
And a heart full of light
I stand beneath the full moon
Praying things will turn out right

@sgr_writing

Sophie Cook

this: is a moment of crisp leaves
sinking
curling and twisting
crimped to the soft airs edge
in a plummet thinking

they drift through harsh
air - so bleak
our rhythms syncing

this is unwelcoming
but so inviting
somehow such a relief to breath in
this is a sort of renaissance
fighting tired snowflakes
crisp leaves and the getaways
that say
we just want to be caught
the fall is cold
and the landing is colder
s.c
- fall conversations

@writingsophie

The Last Time
Lily Rosemary

As a little girl I looked up
to you. You were this strong,
tall and confident man that
could take on the world. Those
amazing blue eyes, the smell
of cigarettes around you. But
as the years flew by, things
took a turn; cancer.

And I remember, when you
rested your head down for the
last time, you didn't look like
the man you used to be. Suddenly
you seemed small and vulnerable.
And I knew, you would never
open those beautiful blue eyes
or light a cigarette ever again.

@lilyrosemary_

06 28 20

J.R. Taylor

Cool Monday summer morning,
my dog stops to take a shit in my neighbors lawn.

I hear clapping
I look around confused
until I saw the window open on the second floor
and the sudden addition of:
"FUCK"
    "FUCK!"
        "FUCK!"
not the
'I-just-stubbed-my-toe-FUCK!-
                FUCK!-
                FUCK!'

my dog awkwardly makes eye contact with me.
"Knock it off," the dog says
as if I was the one making the noise,
"I'm trying to poop here!"

I shrug at the dog
and urge her to hurry up,
there is so much beauty in this shit-
"FUCK!"
    "FUCK!"
        "FUCK!"
- I was uncomfortable.

The dog finishes
and we walk away-
the clapping falling quiet behind us.

At home I feed the dog and crawl into bed.

She runs her fingers through my hair,
"What you thinking about?"

"Taking you from behind," I reply.
"You?"

She laughs,
"McDonald's. I'm hungry."

@@j.r.taylor_writes

Sweet Escape
Rita Serra

Wearing milk mustaches as a disguise
Under King size bed cover we hide

Our crime: stealing a moment in time

Dropped crumb trails will tell the tale of escapade
Can't hide our 1AM Pepperidge Farm raid

Not a price, I wouldn't pay to live this moment twice

Making a daydream of a sleepless night
My darling your are better than morning light

@ritaontherocks

Always a better Time
Barbara Soehner

Somewhere my mind says
There is always a better time
I gently remind myself
Don't fall down inside your heart
Don't hide...

brightness is definitely
Somewhere
My mind says, Really!!!
Oh well lately it's been dark
I gently remind myself

There is always a better time

@barbara_soehner

Death Note
Joanne F. Blake

Speaking from beyond, never knew
they would not wake
Descended up in heaven, on a call
that God didn't make
Holding open sessions, remembering
the last words they spoke
All sent down to loved ones,
on a little black Death Note

@joannethepoetess

climb
Laura Mackennon

We climb shut-the-fuck-up mountain
together
and I'm a kid on Christmas Day in July
because anger is just hope// an unfinished
highway bridge between reality
and expectation.
climb.
I used to think the absence of anger meant love
because I grew up in a house on fire
(but I'm fine now and that's not true).
climb.
I tell you that I'm a poet because my
tolerance for humiliation is high.
I traded normal-sized reactions for
sentimentality in a Moroccan market
climb.
so when you seethe livid silence i
am belt buckles dripped in honey.

@silkstanza

Haiku: Rain
Isabelle Chow

Pitter Patter Rain
Plinking on the windowpane
Cold Weather Warm Heart

@singing_scratchpoet

Everything's Fine.
Sean Murphy

kids,
dinner's ready!

"where's daddy?"

daddy's just been out
in the garage.

utensils ping against plates.
invisible pins drop in the spaces
between a mother
and her unsuspecting children.

"he's been out there
a really long time."

car engine running.
mother's indifference
sloshes in her wine glass.
a floorboard creaks.

...

"do you smell smoke?"

sit down and eat your vegetables.
your father's busy.

smoke alarms going off.
not another word is said.

@seanfrancismurphs

Boredom Study
Kalah McLaughlin

A Polaroid picture pierced
with a thumbtack
on a cork board

The purple quilt my
grandmother made for me
strewn across the couch

A layer of dust on the tv

Headphones knotted on the
dresser

Goosebumps rising on my
arms from the draft of an
open window

The chill of being alone
/of wasted space/

@kalahehm

Kate Gombert

Up to my neck

full moon holding me in still waters
I try to think
to listen
to the birds flying away from the impending storm

Up to my neck

I sink below the moon touched pool
and give to her the tears I have to shed
and surface again as waves hold me hostage

Up to my neck

@kategombert_

Adittya Raj Jain

humility in its deepest form
often proves alternatively

instead of appreciating the person
people tend to live in a shell so formed

they start believing them as superior
and not the privileged being of modesty

@nikasha_belief

Topography
Ryan Sam Turner

Under the cold sheets
hot water bottles keep us warm.
We are cocooned together;
I can feel your heat.
My hands move around
your faultless form,
while my mind scans and traces
the topography of your perfection.

@ryansamturner

Garden of the Gods
Tahlia Durrant

Jewels of
blush
adorn the
strawberry bliss,
her layers of
petal silk,
an alluring
abyss,
touched by
Apollo,
bound by a
fragrant kiss.

@apricotdaisies

Production Costs

Ryan Sam Turner

I am the origin of my own misery –
only me;
continuously recycling my dejection.

The idiosyncrasies of my character
that once seemed endearing,
now enslave me –
all-consuming.

Whispers in my brain
repeat, repeat,
instructing me to do things
that often displease.

Too weak to disagree
with the disobedient cerebrum
inside me,
I am forced to obey.

After each poor decision
I am left shamefaced
and shattered,
lambasting myself with
bitter reproaches.

Anger and hypertension
swell and squeeze
while my fists clench
and then release.

Hardly able to breathe,
I bite my lip,
until blood appears.
It feels like I'm free.

@ryansamturner

118

Body and Stardust
Anjali Chaturvedi

you hate the way your stomach rolls look

in a bodycon dress

and the way your stretchmarks look

as you complain about not wearing a mini skirt

and you continue to blabber about

how your acne covers your whole face

but baby girl, have you ever seen your smile while you talk about poetry

or your eyes while you explain a conspiracy theory

or your laugh when you crack a funny joke yourself?

have you, baby girl?

because if you did, you would know

people are not antiques in the museum

they are humans and what set us all apart

is how different our souls are

and yours is made up of gold and stardust.

The sun has almost left.
Sammi Yamashiro

In this block of cement
where impermanence lives,
there are brief little visits
of the light's sunkiss.

It happens 'round mid noon:
the blinds create their stripes;
sun rays sting the dirty windows
and unveil some floating life;
and with it, silence brews.
Ah...
Silence...

In a home where chaos is constant,
the quiet is the blanket that lulls me to sleep.
It's the calm before the inevitable storm.
I shut my eyes to shield the nightmare dream,
but this barrier, so paper thin, can only do so much for me.

@sammiyamashiro

"who are you 'cause you're not the girl i fell in love with"

your words hit me like bullets, one by one, right in the chest and suddenly i was paralysed, unable to move, unable to comprehend the hate escaping your mouth. i just could not understand how you could blame me for changing when the person standing in front of me was a stranger. you said that i was different now but you were the one that i could not recognise. it hurt me like an open wound, burned me, to see your eyes, once so passionate and familiar, staring back at me now with such indifference as if they had never gazed upon me so longingly before. maybe because you had morphed into someone new so you saw me through a stranger's eyes and when i showed you the mirror so you could see the deception you had become, you burnt red hot with rage and let a string of profanities spill out of your once perfect mouth. was it because you could not handle the fact that you were to blame and that you had never been particularly good at owning up to your mistakes, or did you just wake up one day and decided you hated me so much so you peeled off your skin and unleashed the monster inside you in hopes that i would blame myself for loving you.

@thelies_wetell

[ ] (**placeholder**)
Naproud Cherchawankul

don't worry, honey
it's not you, it's just your face
that I borrowed as a placeholder
for the one that I guess I just haven't seen yet
so be a guest, welcome,
in the house in my head for tonight
and if the phone rings; I'll place you on hold
knock at the door; I'll hold you in place
because really don't worry, honey,
it's not you, just your face
spread wholly on the table as a place mat,
I weighed it down with its own set of cutlery and a plate
so do it, come claim it as yours, break into this space
- I'll tell you a secret, I forgot to lock the back gate -
welcome to the house in my head where I'm holding you a
place
ask me if you'll hold a place
in the pace of my heart and my fate.

@hypnicthoughts

Warbling Heart
Robert Dominick

We sway,
Our laughter like music on the air,
And I realize:
All these notes
Stave off for a moment
The inroads that Time makes;
Those convertible top-down singalongs
Wield a mystifying power,
Those diner jukebox jam sessions
Let us slice out a sliver of memory
And replay it
To our heart's content;
Maybe those echoes
Sing the song of our lives,
That warbling melody
That makes the path ahead
A little less scary.

@realrobdompoetry

sink and swim

Loraine De Lumen

the days add up
until it dilutes the grief
that still lingers
it's as if i've held my breath
underwater for so long
that once i resurfaced
breathing life back into my lungs
i was also breathing in
the sharp scent of misery
you left behind
yet -
i find that swimming
against the current
did not always prove
to be a losing battle.

@lorainewrites

cold skin, empty soul
s.t. tuchin

you were the one that i could count on
when my faith in the world disappeared.
you were the one that i relied on
late at night when i couldn't sleep.
my heart would smile when you called me
but now that's only in my dreams.

one night alone,
and we've changed.
we once would lie awake and dream together,
but now we only lie.
i used to feel your breath
on my neck
in the dark when
the starlight stirred me.
my skin is cold,
my soul is empty.
these blankets cover me,
yet i lie here freezing.

this comforter i surround myself with
drowns me in its irony.

@reservoirsummer

Blushing in my dreams
Sophie Cook

speckles of warm orange spitting from a dimly lit bulb
she closes her eyes, each eyelash gently resting on its bed
for the day.

a meeting of oceans
pacific and atlantic
underneath crimson skies -
nightly and ever so slightly
these bouncy grass blades dream
with caution
until the clouds part again

and a brighter orange always comes
intruders in her pastel sunset world
a fruit bowl of shades melting
into each others arms

when eyelashes dream
they always receive
the sides of her mouth crinkle
upwards tonight
and under the freckling light
her smile gleams

s.c

@writingsophie

Weather
Osama Waheed

Whatever Weather is. Autumn is spreading inside.

@omswritings

hungry hills
Z.

sky burns,
a melancholic peach
juicy and fragrant
while the hungry hills feast
on my morality
and with every imperfect stride
of my malnourished step,
i continue to search for
your lips in hers

@theearnestpoet

Junkie Child

Brandon White

When she walked into the gas station,
I wasn't sure what I was seeing.
Orange hair, white button-up shirt,
jean's too long for her legs
but long enough to pad her
shoeless feet,
hunched over in some
unearthly angle.

She placed a large can of beer
by the register
and laughed
at a joke only she knew.
She turned to me
and straightened her back,
revealing her sore-covered face
and brown teeth.

I stared into hopeless eyes.
The eyes of the damned.
Filthy, drugged out of her mind-
barring some miracle,
all that's left is the dying.
Someone held her as a child-
or maybe they didn't.
Someone should've.

She smiles
like a
sunset.

@brandonwhitemusicandpoetry

Information is Education
Stephanie Langley

The News
Tells you what
They want you to hear
Mainstream
Bias
Bigotry
You think you're educating yourself
But you're just eating up their schpiel
Force fed information
When there's a whole world out there
You think you're exploring it
But the reality is
Manipulation of the grandest scale
Group think
Orchestrated by that top 1%.

@rhyming.s.lang

pretty please
Prynne Argo

lilypad hopscotch
fairy dust blush
keep me in your pocket
pick me pick me pick me
never out of touch.

@prynne.poetry

Smiles of Yesteryear
Srijani Chatterjee

The morning reels in another new beginning
Black coffee brews on the kitchen counter

She muses as she perches
Trailing a finger across her jaw till
The unison of her hand meets her temple

Sighing
Into the tedium of routine

And it's not till
Her back is broken
Her eyes weighed down

That she pauses and glances
At the photograph on the mantle
Stationary as the smiles of yesteryear

Framing a time that could move slow

@srijaniwrites

Tanya Wasyluk

you are home. blueberry jam.
though i never thought i'd find myself by
getting lost in a man.
you are a well-loved book
on a sunday afternoon. spring chimes
in the wind and the magic of the moon.
and d a r l i n g, that look you give
from the other side of the room.
and there are fights. and sometimes tears.
but everything we've said,
there is forgiveness in our hearts
as we unravel in the bed.

@w0nTan

Leah Fricke

I am all
Fluttering heart and hands
itching
to hold a warm body;
stomach aching
(appetite insatiable)
for love
in each and every form.
What a
cavernous space
I have created
inside my ribcage
for somebodys
who were
never meant
to dwell there.

@when.sunshine.rains

A. S. Lindén

today i put the coffee to brew
and sat down with my roommate
we converse, ask each other how were doing
and then i go and say it
voice trembling, hands shaking

i think ive got no choice but leave
i love you, i love this place,
but i feel like i cant take it anymore

i think i just broke up with my roommate

why does no one talk about the pain
of leaving your friends,
the home youve built
the life youve lived?

how does one just leave that?
why do i do this to myself
over and over again?

@mypillowpoetry

landmarks
Madison Sylvester

i walked through my neighborhood today
it is not the same as it was before
but on every corner there remains
a landmark of us

the furniture store we window shopped at
(and imagined buying a fruit bowl
for thousands of dollars)
is closed now
but the bar we stepped into
(and promptly stepped out of
to have a beer in bed instead)
had their doors wide open

then i walked into my apartment
and every inch was a landmark of us
i couldn't cross the street
to avoid a thought of you

@madisonmusing

Acquired taste
Kendry Poetry

She's an acquired taste.
A creamy saltiness at first bite,
to whet one's appetite.
Nectarous hints in ensuing mouthfuls,
leaving you insatiable.
This palate, forever changed.

@kendrypoetry

I Wore my Scandals to the Party
Rajat Bhargava

I wore my scandals to the party, anxiety on one foot and
depression on the other.
Everyone was wearing proper foot attire, but my feet were
tired and I wanted to be comfortable.
All my relatives and family friends were there, and they'd
all had their coat of arms dry-cleaned;
Slowly sipping chai, they gossiped about my last post,
which shed light on my brain's brownout.
A brown boy had come out and sprung into the sea of
scrutiny, hoping to be a lighthouse
For others who also had sinking relationships with
themselves, and didn't want to drown.
"So scandalous" they muttered, and I felt scantily dressed
with everyone's spotlight on me.
Their eyes bore holes in my bare skin, ushering me to
address the elephant in the room;
So I climbed upon the elephant, and started rotating
around the different social circles there.
We were greeted with no fanfare, as we were widely
regarded as an unspectacular circus act.
"One mustn't romanticize their issues openly. They're not
public affairs." said a spectacled uncle.
"It's unfair of you to speculate that they're love affairs in
my mind's private quarters." I countered.
"I wish they'd go away. I've hid them like a magician that's
mastered a disappearing coin trick.
I've coined my anxiety and depression Bonnie and Clyde,
they've stolen so much from me.
So before giving one's two cents, one ought to spend some
time thinking things through.
Saying my truth freed me, maybe leading others to
breakthroughs with their inner incarceration".
I dismounted, and all were astounded, bewildered at how
I'd domesticated this feral animal.
There was not a single sound, dead silence, besides the
strident striding of my scandals.
Each step wore them out, and they began to buckle as my

feet continued to press on them;
I started surmounting them, slowly but surely, and I
consoled those overcome with emotion.
Some people were looking down, perhaps ashamed of how
they'd looked down on me before.
All of a sudden, my anxiety kicked in, and I felt them aim
their eyes at my scandals, judging my mental again.

@mystipheye

On Summer
Zachary J. Ferrara

Sun-kissed
the scent of Coppertone
in the air
I watch as sweat
pools in the small of your back
you hand me a cigarette
Bowie on the radio
a meddling bee overhead
the distinct chatter
of neighbors
through an open kitchen window
turning book pages
in unison
seemingly content

@zjfwriter

The Sunday News
Ferial Mohamed

Sunday mornings are not made for being
alone. I can feel this well enough in my
sternum. Still there is pleasure in late sleep.
Wake up in the waist of the sun's body, poach

an egg scrambling itself while I'm trying not
to break the yolk. A missing lover not present
to testify to underwilted spinach. Someone not
in the kitchen offering to warm my coffee getting
cold too quick while I'm reading the paper.

The Paper:
People dying right here in Africa. So close to me.
War in the Middle East, a man with my last name
massacred. I stay alive. An earthquake in the

Phillipines. Volcanoes. After breakfast a quiet walk, a
quick drive down to the sea with the radio DJ's voice
soothing stone still silence. A nap later, some gardening,

the unwinnable task of keeping an orchid in bloom,
the lonely day's joy swimming in the mire, my old
jazz records, the original kind from New Orleans,

happy unplagued solitude, somewhat. Before sunset
read the news again, sleep a vacant sleep, understand
the privilege of loneliness is a fine piece of luck.

@ferial.poetry

Memories.
Patricia-Ana Dujic

Take me away from here.
Let me forget the worries and blur my memories so that
only dust remains of them.
Adorn me with new colours.
Adorn me with the treasure of the gods and let me shine in
the silky glow of the unconscious.
Because it is so much easier to dance without a burden.

Odvedi me odavde.
Da zaboravim brige i zamaglim uspomene tako da ostane
samo njihova prašina.
Voli me novim bojama.
Voli me bogatstvima bogova i dopusti mi da sijam u
svilenom sjaju nesvjesnog.
Jer je puno lakse plesati bez tereta.

Bring mich fort von hier.
Lass mich vergessen die Last und verwische meine
Erinnerungen sodass nur noch Staub von ihnen übrig ist.
Ziere mich mit neuen Farben.
Schmücke mich mit dem Schatz der Götter und lass mich
erstrahlen im seidigen Glanz des Unbewusstseins.
Denn es lässt sich unbeschwert soviel leichter tanzen.

@p_tizia

MIDNIGHT FLASHBACKS
Matthew Gutierrez

I interacted with the dark street
rain washing clean the sins of a careless world
my memory transported to a time
when I was a life-hungry adolescent.

Summer nights with the neighborhood children
two and five houses down
friendships produced through coincidence
and identical zip codes, fatalism.

Light poles illuminating the endless games of ghost and
tag
love producing touches, chasing your current crush
through foolish dreams of white dresses and tuxedos.

Time a construct, two hands on a clock,
midnight struck twice as the parental power
screamed my name through the thin air
and ignorant bliss, seeping from the laughter of children.

Parting of ways, secret handshakes
smitten eye stares at the neighbor girl
offering up, a see you later
when the sun greets me through the second story window.

Careless and free
I hold to unforgettable memories as water cleans the city
I often lack the power to live in the moment
the dark street loves to remind me, of days that use to be.

@notes2poetry
@matthewjames_g

Leah Fricke

I met a bird
who sang so
sweetly.
She taught me
all her songs.
When I sat down
to compose my own,
the words came out
all wrong.
I found a tune
that fit my tongue
and hummed it
all day long,
but the only way
it made any
sense
was when your
name
was sung along.

@when.sunshine.rains

Lines
Sophie Louisa Stephens

Solvent tulips,
Distilled in a cup,
Stasis,
I watch them puff,
Like my swollen eyes,
Growing pains, from stretching,
Can I change? Will I ever?
Stems broken at the bottom,
Tired of this shit,
Other people hold success like bullet points with each
blink,
I sit and scribe the world, keeping to the deepening lines of
my pondering forehead.

@fringepoetry

Clem Loris

just like
an ice cream headache
you happened
and then you were gone

leaving me
holding my temples
wondering what the fuck
is going on

@clem_loris

Homestay
lydia falls

you gifted me a comb as if
your message had been written
in a neat and surly script:
how my hair was far too ragged
and i was surely not your orphan
or the image you had wished
upon your family— begrudgingly,
i brushed my hair with tangled fingers
and held my breath in desperation
when i wandered in the carpark
holding hands with wide-eyed
strangers and i was only
twenty-two and i was allowed
to feel in love and i was allowed
to search for truth in
foreign presence

@lydiafalls_

//**s e l e n e**
the poetess

rays

of light/
ly

kiss the tips

of
i n c a n d e s c e n t
fin
gers

when she cradled
the moon

in the palms
of her
h a l l o w e d
hands

@the.poet.s

Crimson Ruby Amber
Vrinda V. K.

Wicked winds whisper
Cool touch sending shivers
As crackling grounds snap
Dried leaves like paper

Craning far and away
The fingers of the forest splinter
Their fate to remain asunder
Stumbling over roots and creek
In search of magic and wonder

Little beating hearts scurry
Foraging 'fore a dark, hard battle
Neither triumph nor yet fall
But quiet as cats in nature's hall

She rests after a long Summer day
The pale maiden tossing Her violent, flaming hair
Warmth reflected in eyes that hold fire
And dust sprinkled on Her sweet skin

When oozing ribbons of gold wither
She closes Her eyes silent and eager
Preparing for Winter's cold slumber
Dreaming of Her tragic, frosty lover

Fevered anticipation of His red caress
Waiting in dark cheer tending Her tress
A tale of crimson ruby amber
The colours of Autumn's daughter

@cinderconecrucible

Bumblebees & Their Secrets
Kathryn Kluttz

The hum the buzz deep inside the
nectarous castle of honey the crescendo
the cacophony for bumblebees have
secrets too of sweet sugar served on the
veranda at noon or the spill of coffee
from the flaxen haired lady on the patio,
mind gardens plump with growth rose
bud blossom that plighted troth or
gardenias that are aromatic and attract a
mass of buzzing bees that feed from her
sweet palms until blood is drawn for
their vital secret is the draining of
nectar from the loins of those blooms
that sprout until they are sucked dry
and the hum the buzz in indicative
indeed of their secret language that only
the bumblebees know.

@hailspoetry

144

There are Things You Will Never Know
Nick Thiel

filling in the empty symbols with meanings
lonely is love coming in
from the cold
you can't have your cozy any other way
elchemical desolation trick
you must be running
through your mind wild
because I never see
your hieroglyphic thought films
and I miss
sitting uncomfortably in shitty restaurants and bars
finding G_d was the easy part
you and I didn't know where to go from there
so I kept coming home
with flowers and desires
but there was no language being spoken in any room
only the glare campaign
too many times
there were two of you
I was never clear about the time she left
I sat shivering
couldn't get cold
on the border of beginnings
baseball games
coach pitch
under these beautiful evil
fluorescent pillars
I am a stranger passing through
on pilgrimage to the other chapel of fluorescent hell
7/11
it's summer and people are talking fall

@midwestandblessed

burnout
Kimberly Cramer

cold water thrown
over burning embers
purpose squeezed out
like a wet rag for drying

@k.a.c._writes

Fate Painter
Donna Eli

We could cut red threads
blocking our way
or we could gallop in every strand,
either way,
we still have hair to frizzle
and colour in whatever we want
and still consider this as fate
smeared on our thumbs.

@bydonnaeli

waking glaze
Caitlan Docherty

the sky bakes
honey dawn
the sun dresses
morning

orange juice spilled
peach flesh squeezed
strawberry seeds of
decoration

memories slurred
eyelids still heavy
fresh thought yet
to pour through

@cmnpoetry

disintegration
M J

we walk down the street and each time
you find a penny on the ground
you put it in your shoe
it will bring good luck you tell me
and i laugh because i think
it is adorable that you believe in magic
we walk down the street and each time
you find a penny on the ground
you put it in your shoe
stop wasting my time you hear me say
and i yell because i think
it is stupid that you believe in magic
we walk down the street and each time
there is a penny on the ground
you pass by it without looking down
and as we walk together in silence i realize
that without the pennies in your shoes
we are out of luck

@sleeplessmind

Mother of Mine
Srijani Chatterjee

She was born into second place
A gender default she could not
Merely live to overcome

Much like her mother before her
Succumbing to a subordinate life
As if compensation was due

For being born a secondary race

To the race of men that ruled
The sphere of women where
Even her mother before her

Was but a mere race horse

Out of the race for not bearing
A mare

Out of the race for not bearing
An heir

@srijaniwrites

149

day and night, in a blender
David McIntyre

All I want right now
is a quiet drink
in a tranquil bar
waiting for the storm
to give up or pass
so I can stumble home
under the clearing sky
to sleep off the drunk
boredom of running dry.

@sisterkind

Pyjama stains.
Kirsten Deane

My pyjama pants have nail polish stains
from when I tried to be a better woman
with a stiff hand and a skew wrist.
I look down and see my sticky desperation-
It's stuck to my skin and crawled its way onto
my clothes.
Black and pink and brown,
a subtle pretty because that's what counts,
the sight of a secret attempt.

@breathing_poetry

Purple
Diane Lato

Wine sitting on the roof of your tongue / a little too young /
like a frisky pony not ready for the tracks / but when she is
/ oh she'll be the best

The heart of a 30-something / yours, maybe / bruised but
still beating

A French kiss laced with mixed berries / clasped hands in
the shade of full-bloom lilacs / faint yet / intoxicating

An old velvet gown / drawn from an even older drawer /
smelling of sea salt & lavender / thick & ethereal like the
night sky / beneath your fingers / softer than the stars
you've heard so much about - but never seen

The ocean wrapping your bare feet / the only rings you'll
ever need / murmuring a siren's song / "if only i could see
this" / the moon feels so bright you can almost see her /
with your eyes wide open / she feels full, but not quite / (not
quiet) / like you

@diane_writes

I will never

James Kinsella

I will never ~~~~
I will never have a woman's flesh to hold
or inner beauty to fall deeply in love with
once more. That part of my life to love
and behold is over.

I will never have another chance to look
my sweetheart in their eyes and tell them
how beautiful they are.

I will never hold a lover's rosy cheeks in
my hands and kiss their lips hello.

I will never hold my dearest love so tight
that I feel their heart beating next to
mine, and the warmth from their skin
escapes and touches my skin, warming
mine.

I will never taste heartwarming teardrops
as they touch my lips, quenching the
thirst I have inside. To elevate my heart to
those upper emotions that I discover in
that warmth from those droplets falling.

My hands will never hold the hands of a
woman, and I will never dance to a tune
that brings two hearts together. My heart
will never meet and blush at the songs
sung by a woman's heart.

My fate has taken me to a death, a death
of loneliness. For the moment, I know
that I will never experience the touch of a
woman and her blessedness. My mind is
clear, and I am heartbroken, my spirit has
no opportunity to discover a home for its
restlessness.

My soul wants to depart this life knowing
the reality of my destiny, but my time is
not up, so here I am uttering these few
words from my lips, "I will never."
Knowing this keeps me empty and alone
looking for the day I could discover
solace for my heart in the unknown.

@jim.akinsel.1

5am
Carol G

this feeling that i have inside
i can't express the words
it's 5am all over again
i clearly hear the birds.

@cgxpoems

153

Milestone
lydia falls

he brought up the green
that used to coat my walls
like a child wailing for redemption;
i swore it was the way
i was raised (frozen from lime-
light yet still starving for
attention) and it was never
aggression i had known but
the subtleties of how words clink upon
words, striking at emboldened bones
like the keepsake of a child:
thought-struck and mesmerized
by the dull creak in knees or the
thrum beyond dusk or the
silence between dialogue (faint yet
everpresent);
        so i took that measure
and weighed out all my paperbacks
in hopes that prose outgrows the hollow,
carving out a cold fifteen, arrested
for theft— i left the herbs in the car like
evidence seared in stone, clutching
at my notebook, grasping for the phone:
my mother is in the Philippines and
my father in the city and could we
please come to an agreement (on our
own)?
    well i could never break the spell
of birdsong, but i was told to shut my mouth
before i mispronounced my verbs
and this is where they found me: in a crinkled
plastic bag, enchanted with the mysteries that
kept me inside out; it's pistachio shells, they said—
then let me off with less, only waking to a world
where sunlight pours into a vessel like
a damp and heavy sweat, still grief-stained and
empty, grasping for regret; so later that week

i bought buckets of paint
and sloshed on
all that baby green—

the way the hue forgave me
with its teeth marks in my skin,
dull and thin yet aching,
strewn up and down my ribcage
like a milestone sculpted from bark:
burrowed in its camouflage,
yet pleading for a shade
to fill the vacant

@lydiafalls_

callouses
Jessica Paige Ballen

we make blood oaths from our noses
sitting in silence to the pressure of sad songs
I still lick sides of soda cans for the bacteria
passing street names like Shotgun Lane
with lost dog flyers for a beast named Buster
there's a cancer in this tropical heat
and driving East only makes me bitter
June bugs in July suffocate against my pillow
casually watching sundaes melt on a Monday
telling time just got a little harder
I tell you that moms and therapists hate me
and I can't quit wearing black lipstick to sleep
if you're not here for the sore throats
idk what you came here to see

@sirenleech

home
Elowen Grey

i don't know how
to name this need that grips me
roots severed // lost of soil
call it ribs in want of space to reach
call it a flicker of life
little hands that reach for each other
response unsure

     unsteady

and all i've ever wanted
is a home that is not mine

to sit in witness

     breathe

flowers from seeds
he planted // and grew me

grandfather's hands
built and entire world
burned and buried
by the greedy and grabbing
hands of time

     and men

and I sit in this moment
eyes closed

     pretending

that thousands of miles
do not actually separate
me from this place
that the soil in my hands

is ready to hold the seed of my life

that i don't need to stretch across
an ocean to feel the pulse
because i carry it inside of me
always beating

      i am not lost
          i am leaning

{home}

@elowengreypoetry

Autumn
Deonna Marie Ferreira

Autumn steals into my heart
cold and crisp
like morning fog
and I crumble
under a flannel blanket.
My efforts for warmth
are in vain.

@deonna.marie.poetry

Vicariously
Samantha Sankar

I remember being his flower –
Sitting out on the cobbled stoop
Where he left me,
My happiness at the mercy of the sun,
Until I withered, and fell apart,
My scorched petals brushing against
The dust of the ground.
He piled my death into his palms
And put them in the bind of a romance novel,
With sullen eyes,
To live vicariously through its words.
He cared for them fervently.
He cared for them
A little too late.

@r.s.samantha

A trip to the shops while thinking about you
Uniliar L

Concrete pavement with lines that reach small trees of
bonsai,
waving like in a theatre through the fences. Hearing the
orchestra sew
notes through the earbuds connected to my phone, turning
the sky aqua
to the orange that dispersed sun dust as I went within.

Shelves that line fruits and vegetables, with packets of
sweet
and I walk through the aisle, sugar smiles contagious from
the smell of tea.
Scanning through mangoes and strawberries, three should
be enough.
I zip up the hole, heading around the corner where an
owner and Shih Tzu
took their walks every Sunday night. The dog fetching a
twig

and my bag filled with memories. When we walked pass
the lake in a loop,
laughing at the misdirection, paths held together like the
pages in a novel.
Illumination of the streetlight that glowed the same
as the intersection of the train station to the road.
Remembering the smell of vanilla
from the cupcakes, and you wanted the one with choc
chips.
The weight of this glitter is my never-ending adventure.

@orange.inspire

Mushroom
Afreeca Daniel

It didn't exist yesterday.
It appeared today however.
This morning when I stepped out my door,
It was there.
A mushroom.

An ordinary dark brown
Like a smutch of moist mud on
Casual boots
Nothing special.

I wondered why it decided to build a home here.
Here in filt and pollution.
A void of endless frustration.
It will surely return to the earth the next time I see it.
The merciless sun embarking on
The horizon will surely kill it.

I left.
The clouds came out.
A thick dark grey pulled the covers
And tucked in the mushroom.

And So...
It lived.
In this place of filt and pollution.
Thriving in negative emotions.
It stood small and proud.
Fighting the rain.
One could say, welcoming it.

Like I had welcomed all the mornings before this one
It was there the next day.
And the weeks following.
Never growing a little.
Just living.

After I had cleaned up the outside.
Pulling up weeds, loosing the soil.
It's ordinary color even more typical
A light grey.

When I could finally breathe again,
I gave it a bit of water

Bearly a few drops.
The next day,

It returned home.

@freekah_mali

a crime scene
Anahi boyar

She was damaged
like a crime scene
Restricted to enter,
too mysterious,
she had questions
that only she could answer
and the trauma was
something she didn't ask for,

@and.the.stars.cried

WOW

Barbara Soehner

Wow
No one is in sight
The street is quiet
Not a whisper can be heard
Not even a lonely singing bird

Wow
I have a tiny bit of fright
But I am brave
No one is around to enter
This cave in my mind

So I search and wonder
What is to come
Just had to get out
Walk a bit before
I become undone

Wow
No one in sight
Where is everyone
What is going on
Behind so many
sHuttered windows
Behind so many
closed doors

Wow
Lights are
shining inside
They must be
having fun
People drawing closer
Healing has begun

@barbara_soehner

what the weeds sing
Caitlan Docherty

promise me i
am beautiful
left
unpicked and
untended

on roadside
in your garden
sprouting
feebly through
a crack
in pavement

think of me
often
unfixed and
lovely
out of sorts
and stranger
to arrangement

let me
be
unbent by
unkind
hands or
feet or
accidents

hold me
close
but never
pull
me
from home

@cmnpoetry

Midsummer's Gold

Rosslyn Chay

The first wave washes over the fields,
rousing the maidens already primed
to bathe in the nurturing warmth of dawn.

Shying not from the limelight, they spread—
glorying in their perfect whorls,
welcoming the furry suitors

to rest in their bosoms.
No haste needed on this southern day
to master the waggle

and harvest the ambrosia,
then passing it on—from one
to another; from nectar to honey to wax.

As the orb draws its longest arc from east to west,
a drop of gold find its home
in the cell of a comb.

@voicesofyun

O To Live, O To Die
Kathryn Kluttz

o to fight / o to speak / o to live / o to die /
these are the sorrows that overtake the land /
and help us survive / so clench your fists /
and scream / into the heavens / and weep for
the forgotten souls / that rage in the belly of
the fire burning sky / eaten away by the
flames / o to burn / o to perish / tis a mad
thing you must cherish / the death / the
cleansing / of this planet / o to cease / o to
succumb / to the eager hungry sky that rains
down atrocious atrocities upon the world / so
rage on into that cold dawn morn / and come
back renewed by the fire / your flesh burned
and torn / for you will arise stronger / from
the blazing sun / there is death as there is life.

@hailspoetry

intrusive thoughts
lindy v.h

fuck,
calm down calm down calm down
i tell myself when the first intrusive thought attacks
but it's too late, i am not in control
the sound of their voices growing thicker
smothering the air around me
distressing memories of words and whispers
bashing in the inner doors of my mind
i try to swallow and ignore the huge pit
that grows wider in my stomach with each second
but their eyes try to pierce through me
and my shaking hands give me away
i utter *'i'll be right back'*
and pace to the door to find my way outside

my breath quickens as the images
flash uncontrollably through my brain
body shaking
tears streaming
cheeks tingling
hyperventilating only just kicked in
it feels like the fear is filling up my lungs
choking me with the memory of your words
i sit down on the wooden bench and lean over
my elbows trying to rest on my shaking knees
my eyes trying to focus on the stone tiles below

you're here you're okay you're alright
are the words that i try and focus on in my mind
i press my hands to the ground
i hear the birds chirping
and feel the warm sun on my hair
i inhale and exhale
i guess i'm back to reality
but then why do i not feel any better?
i look at my hand which is still resting on the pavement
while the last teardrop drips down to the floor

i finally am able to bring out words again
and whisper to myself
'i'm not okay' as i walk back to the door

@lindy.v.h

allie n

i can see
the spiderweb cracks,
spreading
across every inch of my heart,
but i know:
no matter how broken our
hearts, our
souls, our
bodies become —
it's just to let the
light shine through.

@ascrittoran

NYC Melancholy

Joan Vargas

Traveling the streets of NYC,
What do I see?
Childhood memories wandering endlessly
Like the spirits Abuela warned me about.
Abandoned on the block searching
For bodies they once called home.
My memories caught sight of me
And took residency.
My NYC.

My childhood jump rope no longer
tapping on concrete.
I gasped, "Just one tap please."
My heart pumping at jump rope speed
As I struggled to breathe.
The fresh air of what once was
Scarcely entered my lungs.
My NYC.

Sidewalk stomping looking for a familiar rhythm.
Hobbies that kept us away from the system.
Emptiness resides where my friends use to stand.
Chanting, stomping and clapping their hands,
"Now give me a beat."
My NYC.

Streetlights weren't forcing me home,
Took off the clothes Abuela had sewed.
Domino tables no longer hovered over the ground.
Where the old man sat with a cigar in his mouth
screaming, "Capicu."
Youngsters would lose and only blessed him with an
"IOU."
My NYC.

"Coco, Cherry, Mango, Rembo"
The coquito man's bell rung.
From where he stood on a corner and sung.

His hustle was something I could never forget,
As he struggled while wiping the sweat from his head.
He charged us two quarters back then,
I stand on his corner looking to find him again.
My NYC.

Living in a neighborhood
Where apartments were about the same size,
Vecinos never shared pies, but surely shared rice.
Our moms bought us the patent leather Reeboks
That were Oh So Fly,
Well at least at the time.

Years have flown by
And everything has passed me.
Yet, I still stand here stagnantly.
I cannot leave, I cannot find peace,
I need to make it back to my NYC.

Damn this NYC Melancholy.

@jav_writes_

In hindsight
Lixin Tan

when i was five,
there was one morning that started with
the ground splitting open and swallowing
my mother.

before that morning,
i never understood being alone and i never
had to pursue my mother like a cat in its
endeavour to trap a light,

or passing strangers trying to catch a glimpse
of each other from opposite sides of a wall,
or my four-year-old self chasing the moon
from inside my father's car, asking why it only

moved further away.
that morning i ran after my mother
as the hem of her skirt disappeared
around the corner of a pillar,

over and over again,
until all the pillars dissolved into the ground
and the sky became a boundless blue, the reach
of my arms, immeasurable.

i grappled with freedom's confusion,
tried to let it settle as i bit my tongue to find the
vocabulary of these strange new emotions—
i know now they were grief, remorse, guilt

as i looked away from the sky
and saw my mother standing on abandoned tracks,
the ballast stones covering up her feet and knees
like all the regrets she kept to herself, sinking,

her arms still as if she never tried grabbing
for the sky. her body flared and receded
into the ground, a quiet fire once bold.
i begged her to take back my life.

that morning i woke up alone in the house.
i was only five but all my dreams were already made;
a yearning for my mother's touch so i knew she was close,
a promise of atonement, unsaid.

@lixin.tan

INDEX

Made in the USA
Middletown, DE
26 September 2020

20140122R00113